Significant Harm:
its management and outcome

Second Edition

Edited by
Margaret Adcock &
Richard White

© Significant Publications, 1998

First published 1991
by Significant Publications
c/o Simpson House
2/6 Cherry Orchard Road
Croydon
Surrey, CR0 6BA

ISBN 0 9518761 3 9

Typesetting by Third Column 0181 892 4255
Print by Spider Web 0171 281 3031

Contents

Contributors

Margaret Adcock is a Social Work Consultant at Great Ormond Street Hospital and a Social Work Trainer.

Arnon Bentovim is Honorary Consultant Child and Adolescent Psychiatrist at Great Ormond Street Hospital for Children and the Tavistock Clinic, and Honorary Senior Lecturer, Institute of Child Health.

David Jones is Consultant Child Psychiatrist and Honorary Senior Lecturer at the Park Hospital for Children, Oxford.

Annie Lau is Consultant Child and Family Psychiatrist at the Child and Family Consultation Centre, Ilford, Essex.

Margaret Lynch is Reader in Community Paediatrics at Guys Hospital, London.

Tony Morrison is a Social Work Consultant and Trainer.

John Simmonds is Senior Lecturer in Social Work at Goldsmith's College.

Richard White is a partner in White and Sherwin, Solicitors, and writer on family law.

Foreword

The first edition of *Significant Harm* was published in 1991 to coincide with the introduction of a new and radical approach to child care in the public sector. Seven years later, lawyers, judges, magistrates together with social workers and the other caring agencies are still struggling to understand and implement the concepts of partnership between social workers and families within the new statutory framework of care proceedings set up by the Children Act 1989.

This second edition, with its invaluable information, comment and advice from distinguished contributors, builds on seven years experience of the working of the Act. It explores the legal and psychological meaning and effect of significant harm and the implications for local authorities. It considers how partnership and collaboration are working both with families and among the agencies and reflects upon the dilemma of too much or too little intervention for problem families.

This is a thoughtful book which explores in depth the problems which continue to arise and are bound to arise from the implementation of the Act. It is, in my view, essential reading for all those, whether judges, magistrates, lawyers, social workers, health care or other professionals, engaged in the difficult, delicate and important task of advising or making decisions about the future of children who have suffered or are likely to suffer from significant harm.

Elizabeth Butler-Sloss
May 1998

Introduction

The provisions of the Children Act 1989 represented a radical change in the thinking about practice and services to children and families and about the way children had been protected since the Children Act 1975. Before 1989 there had been a predominantly 'investigate, rescue and remove' approach to children thought to have been abused or neglected. There was an assumption that 'care' would then provide both the treatment and the solution needed by these children. There was little emphasis on the development of preventive treatment or rehabilitative services and no widely established research and knowledge base about what methods of intervention were effective.

A number of cases in the 1980s which achieved considerable publicity had challenged current practice in two different, and apparently contradictory respects. In some cases, particularly of alleged sexual abuse, as in Cleveland, the Inquiry Report (*HMSO, 1987*) suggested that the local authority had intervened too intrusively in a way that was harmful to children; in other cases, such as Jasmine Beckford and Kimberly Carlisle, the Inquiry reports (*1985 and 1987*) felt there was insufficient recognition of potential danger from the birth family and the child had died at home. At the same time, other cases and research findings (*see Parker et al, 1991 for references*) made it clear that children might experience considerable problems if they came into local authority care. They were losing touch with their families, their attachment needs were not being met, their medical needs were not being attended to, and some were actually being abused in care.

In the debates preceding the 1989 Children Act it was clear that there was a consensus that a new approach to meeting the needs of children was necessary. The Act was intended to create a new balance: children needed to be protected but their long term welfare also had to be promoted. It was felt that in most cases the family would be the best place for the children to be raised, and that parents rather than local authorities should exercise responsibility for their children and decide what was best for them. Local authorities were therefore given responsibilities under Part 3 of the Act to provide support through services for families where children were defined as being in need and, at the same time, under Parts 4 and 5 to provide protection for children suffering, or likely to suffer, significant harm, by investigation and, if necessary, applying to the court for a care or supervision order.

The basic principles that underpin the new Act and the 1991 *Department of Health Volumes of Guidance* are:

- The local authority must work in partnership with parents and assist them to meet their responsibilities.

- There must be a minimum level of intrusion into family life and therefore the grounds for intervention are more specific;

- The possibility of some parents harming their children is recognised and the duty to investigate this is strengthened;

- At all stages in the course of child protection work, even if significant harm is established, consideration should be given to the possibility of working with a voluntary arrangement;

- Courts are enjoined not to make an order unless doing so would be better for the child;

- If a care order is made, local authorities have a duty to return children to their families wherever this is possible;

- Health, education and other agencies have a duty to assist social service departments in the development and provision of both family support services, and child protection.

Defining the new service

Sections 17 and 31 of the Act provide the criteria for both preventive and protective action. They centre on concern about the child's health and development and include both the need for services and the need for protection. Both kinds of service are intended to assist families where the development of the children is or is likely to be impaired. Both section 17, which sets out the duties of local authorities to families of children in need, and section 31, which defines the criteria for care proceedings, refer to the impairment of health or development as the basic condition which must occur or be likely to occur. In working with both sections 17 and 31 social workers will be dealing with children who have suffered, are suffering or are likely to suffer significant harm.

In section 17, a child is defined as being in need if their health or development is likely to be significantly impaired, or further impaired, without the provision of services, or if they are disabled. In section 31 harm is defined as ill treatment or the impairment of health or development. The major difference in definition between the sections is that in section 31 the impairment of health or development must be attributable to unreasonable parental care. Consequently section 31 also enables the Court to make a care order placing the child in the care of the local authority, if it is satisfied that the child is suffering, or is likely to suffer, significant harm and that an order would be better for the child than not making an order. Section 17 enables help to be provided through co-operation with parents: section 31 introduces compulsion, the acquisition of parental responsibility by the local authority, and the possibility of removing the child against the parents' wishes.

The 1989 Act also introduced for the first time the concept of local authority services promoting the healthy development of a child; either within the family or by looking after the child away from the family on a planned basis. Previously local authorities were either striving to keep children out of care until a crisis had been reached or if there appeared to be grounds for care proceedings, focusing almost entirely on the investigation of child abuse and the need to protect children from the abuser. Services were not usually designed to meet the individual needs of the child. Neither the organisation of the services nor the evaluation of their effectiveness focused on the well being or individual outcome for the child, as Jones (*1991*) pointed out in the first edition of this book.

The organisation of preventive and protective services around a central concern for the child's health and development gave local authorities both the opportunity to provide a consistent unified service that met the individual needs of the child and criteria for evaluating the services. It provided a framework for working with significant harm on both a voluntary and a compulsory basis.

The idea of a simultaneous emphasis on partnership with parents, support to families and strong child protection with a minimum reliance on court orders was exciting but it was also untried and untested. Moreover there was, in 1989, no widely-known established research basis to demonstrate what kinds of support services could prevent abuse and neglect in specific family situations. There was also no evidence to suggest that the Department of Health, social services departments, health authorities or education departments recognised the gap that would need to be filled if local authority care was no longer regarded as a therapeutic solution for children who had suffered significant harm.

During the first four years following implementation of the Act in 1991, many other developments occurred which made it difficult for social services to implement the very significant changes in both direction and service provision that the legislators had intended. Both health and education services were reorganised, and the internal market economy became much more prominent. This constrained the development of multi-disciplinary support and treatment provision. The Government placed increasing restraints on public spending and the level of finance available was significantly reduced. Faced with dwindling resources, most local authorities were unable either themselves, or in conjunction with other agencies, to develop a wide range of treatments, interventions, and support services to families with children in need. The focus remained on child protection and access to the limited services available was often through the process of a child protection investigation under section 47 and a case conference rather than through voluntary provision under section 17.

Taking stock: *Messages from Research*

In 1995 the Government published *Child Protection: Messages from Research.* This document set out the key messages arising from 20 research studies. Not surprisingly, because of the context in which the Act was being operated, the findings suggested that there was too much emphasis being placed on child protection and too many cases were being investigated. The research suggested this could cause considerable suffering to families but no legal action might result and the families might not even receive any services. *Messages from Research* highlighted the fact that some of the researchers queried the effectiveness of the investigation process. However, the study by Farmer and Owen (*1995*) showed that children who were the subject of child protection conferences subsequently received significant protection and help. There was also concern that there were some families who appeared to have high levels of need but no substantiated child abuse, and who were not being offered support services. The researchers described families in which there was domestic violence and where there was an atmosphere of high criticism and low warmth but no help was provided.

Messages from Research concluded that, at the time the research was undertaken, the balance between services was unsatisfactory. "The stress upon child protection investigations and not enquiries, and the failure to follow through interventions with much needed family support prevented professionals from meeting the needs of children and families". As a solution it was suggested that "an approach based on the *process* of section 47 enquiries and the *provision* of section 17 services might well shift the emphasis in child protection work more towards family support. A more balanced service for vulnerable children would encourage professionals to take a wider view. There would be efforts to work alongside families rather than to disempower them, to raise their self esteem rather than reproach families, to promote family relationships where children have their needs met, rather than leave untreated families with an unsatisfactory parenting style. The focus would be on the overall needs of children rather than a narrow concentration on the alleged incident."

The Government therefore urged local authorities to see whether it was possible to treat more cases as children in need rather than using the child protection process. This took no account of whether legal proceedings might be the only way to protect the child and also of how families can be helped to change. Compulsion may be perceived as stigmatising to some parents and therefore reduce their ability to co-operate, but for others it may create an impetus for change.

The requirement to re-think policy and practice following the publication of *Messages from Research* led to a vigorous debate amongst professional organisations about the 'refocusing' of children's services. The NSPCC (*1996*) raised a number of important concerns. They said:

- There was a lack of child focus. The emphasis on partnership with parents could operate to the exclusion of the child's perspective;

- The term *low warmth/high criticism* was unclear. The idea that it was a major determinant of poor outcomes was undermined by the lack of definition and the consequent difficulties for practitioners in assessing when it was present;

- Working in partnership was not sufficient on its own to effect change. Specialist services such as comprehensive assessment and therapeutic intervention were essential to good outcomes for many children. The implication in *Messages from Research* that they might not be effective was mistaken and was not backed up by the research studies themselves.

- Some aspects of *Messages from Research* were contrary to other Government Guidance e.g. *Evaluating Performance in Child Protection* (*SSI, 1993*). This left practitioners and managers exposed and vulnerable whatever they did.

The NSPCC suggested that by failing fully to acknowledge the broader influence of diminishing resources, media hostility , and an increasingly managerial and bureaucratic approach to the delivery of services, *Messages from Research* implied that problems could all be remedied by individual practitioners rather than by changes to the system and the way in which this is described and understood.

Refocusing

It was made clear at the Sieff Conference (*Rose, 1996*) that a refocusing of children's services should encompass both child protection and services to children in need. There had to be a balancing of risks, for example in failing to collect crucial evidence for any court proceedings as against intervening in ways which alienate families from the help of Social Services. Understanding harm should be driven less by single incidents and more by the context, including the emotional climate in which the child is living.

At a joint Department of Health and Association of Directors of Social Services Conference in September 1996, the Minster suggested a new five-point strategy for the future:

- Services must be needs-led and designed to meet the needs of children and families rather than fitting them into services;

- Professionals and managers must be cost-conscious and get the best value from available resources;

- There must be a real multi-disciplinary partnership between agencies to build on the success of the *Working Together in Child Protection Guidance* (*1991*) and to ensure that the benefit of such links are applied to all children in need and their families;

- There must be a community-based approach, drawing on local groups and agencies in the community to provide support for families;

- Services should be judged and driven by their outcomes. There needs to be greater clarity about what will be achieved and how far the aims are being realised. Evaluation may often need to be long-term and may not be easy to do. It is not enough to believe that family support works, it needs to be proved. (*1996*) (*Children's Service News 6.10.96*).

The Minister's speech was in some ways a re-statement of the original aims of the Act which had attracted much support in 1989 and had seemed to provide the possibility of offering a much better service to families. However, it posed a major challenge to all organisations and professionals involved with vulnerable children to refocus services to individual children and families to encompass protection, partnership and services to meet needs, with dwindling resources available to do this.

It is not clear how or whether it will be possible to achieve all these aims. The dilemmas which were inherent in the Act in 1989 still remain. There is still little certainty about the best ways of helping families to achieve change and how to help some children achieve their developmental potential. At the same time the context in which help is provided has now worsened. Changes in family structure, the increasing poverty of many families with children, cuts in benefits and lack of adequate child care facilities have placed increasing burdens on vulnerable families and are placing many children's development at risk. Social services departments, health and education services will therefore be faced with trying to meet a rising level of need.

In an evaluation of *Messages from Research*, Parker (*1995*) pointed out that the child protection system, although much criticised, had provided a means of rationing services. Since new responses have to be developed within existing resources and it will not be possible to meet all the demands for services, it will now be essential that a new method of prioritising need is developed.

In spite of the difficulties, many agencies are looking for new ways of multi-disciplinary co-operation and of offering services. The Dartington Research Team (*1995*) has produced useful guidance on matching needs and services, and a framework for developing the Children's Service Plans that the Government now require Social Service Departments to produce. A Department of Health initiative to assess child care outcomes (*1991*) has developed a series of schedules *Looking after Children Materials* (*1995*) to measure the progress of children in care and to assess the quality of care they receive. These initiatives will need, however, to be part of an overall strategy that reflects all the aspects of the refocusing approach and tries to resolve the dilemmas inherent in it.

Bibliography

Department of Health (1995). *Messages from Research.*

Department of Health (1995). *Looking after Children Materials.*

Dartington Research Unit (1995). *Matching Needs and Services. The Audit and Planning of Provision for Children Looked After By Local Authorities.* Dartington.

Farmer, E.,Owen, M. (1995). *Child Protection Practice: Private Risks and Public Remedies.* HMSO.

NSPCC (1996). *Messages from the NSPCC – a contribution to the 'Refocusing Debate'.*

Parker, R. (1995). *Proceedings of the Sieff Conference, 1995.*

Rose, W. (1996). *Proceedings of the Sieff Conference, 1996.*

CHAPTER ONE:

Significant harm: legal implications

Richard White

This chapter considers the concept of significant harm in its legal context, as provided for in the Children Act 1989, in relation to protective measures. The concept applies in duties to investigate or make enquiries, emergency protection and care proceedings under Parts IV and V of the Act. It is related to the definition of 'children in need' under Part III.

Harm is defined in section 31(9) as ill-treatment or the impairment of health or development. Ill-treatment is defined as including sexual abuse and forms of ill-treatment which are not physical, though it must by implication include physical abuse. Health is defined as physical or mental health, and development as physical, intellectual, emotional, social or behavioural development. Children who have or are likely to have impaired health or development come within the definition of children in need.

Significant is not defined in the Act; the *Oxford English Dictionary* defines it as "considerable, noteworthy or important". Volume 1 of *Department of Health Guidance (Court Orders)* states: "Minor shortcomings in health care or minor deficits in physical, psychological or social development should not require compulsory intervention, unless cumulatively they are having, or are likely to have, serious and lasting effects upon the child."

Investigation, enquiries and assessment

A local authority has a statutory duty established by section 47(1) of the Children Act.

"Where a local authority –

(a) are informed that a child who lives, or is found, in their area –

    (i) is the subject of an emergency protection order; or

    (ii) is in police protection; or

(b) have reasonable cause to suspect that a child who lives, or is found, in their area is suffering, or is likely to suffer, significant harm,

the authority shall make, or cause to be made, such enquiries as they consider necessary to enable them to decide whether they should take any action to safeguard or promote the child's welfare."

On an initial referral it may not be clear whether the case concerns a child in need or a child who may be suffering significant harm. Sometimes it may be obvious, but in a case of any complexity it may be difficult to make that decision until some enquiries have been made. It should not be thought that because an initial referral is framed in terms of need or harm, that necessarily dictates subsequent action. The picture should be built up through the making of enquiries. That is not to suggest that a detailed analysis of incidents is necessarily required, rather that an open mind should be maintained on matters. If a social services department is so organised to allocate cases to different sections dependent on criteria, then there must be flexibility in allocation.

The process should ensure that sufficient information is obtained to make an assessment about whether and what action is required. This would include a decision that no action is required, that services should be provided under Part III of the Act or that a further, more detailed investigation has to be carried out, perhaps leading to the provision of services or to civil and/or criminal proceedings. The way in which this process is undertaken will depend on available time, urgency, and what other information is already available.

Attention should also be given to concerns expressed in *Messages from Research* (*HMSO, 1995*) that in many cases enquiries are made which focus narrowly on alleged incidents. If the incident is not proved, the family may receive no services. They may be justifiably resentful and their circumstances may be made worse by the intervention. For the most part enquiries should focus on the needs of the family, provided sufficient attention is given to the possibility that one of those needs may be the immediate or long term protection of the child.

The scope of enquiries and the degree of investigation must be a matter of judgment, but whether there is an assessment of need or an analysis of harm, there should be a clear understanding of the reasons for the provision of a service, which may in some cases require a more detailed investigation. The provision of family support in cases of identified harm is no substitute for clarity as to the circumstances surrounding the harm. Without that it may not be possible to identify the appropriate response to the harm, in terms of proceedings or treatment. Furthermore if care proceedings are necessary, the more detailed investigation will provide the basis of the evidence to substantiate the threshold criteria.

It is equally important to ensure that if there is a need for investigation, that this is not carried out to the detriment of prevention and treatment. Where harm has occurred it may be important to understand the factual basis of the harm to be clear what is being prevented and what treatment is for, but an investigation which has prosecution as its primary focus may well not be appropriate for that purpose. This would suggest the need for a new framework for investigation of those cases which are not to be the subject of prosecution, but may need compulsory measures.

Where there is harm to a child, which may be sufficient to give rise to a decision that proceedings would be initiated, there should be a coordinated analysis of the harm and its causes, undertaken by a team of professionals who can provide the following:

a.   an analysis of the nature of the harm;

b.   an analysis of the likely or possible causes of the harm;

c.   an analysis of the circumstances in which the harm occurred;

d.   an analysis of the consequences of the harm;

e.   an assessment of the carers;

f.   relevant history of the child.

This requires bringing together a group of people with appropriate expertise who together have the ability to provide a composite picture. It is the social worker who has the responsibility to make their own assessment and coordinate the case, but the expertise of the police in investigation and doctors in providing medical opinion will also be necessary.

Guidance will be available from procedures agreed by Area Child Protection Committees and local authority social service departments. Records should be checked. Depending on circumstances it may be necessary to make enquiries of other agencies before there is any contact with the family. If there are injuries, adequate information must be available about their nature and possible cause. A written medical report should be obtained as a matter of urgency, so that there can be no confusion about medical opinion.

Additional information can be gathered from other agencies following a visit, but it should be remembered that the first interview with a carer suspected of causing harm, is likely to be the best opportunity for establishing the most accurate version of events. Thus if medical opinion or other relevant information is available as to circumstances of the harm, that information will be of assistance in carrying out any interviews.

Significant harm may arise in many ways: physical, emotional or sexual abuse or neglect and may be a combination of different aspects. One form may be obvious; another form, such as emotional neglect, may have more harmful consequences, especially in the longer term. It is accordingly important to avoid an excessive focus on one aspect of the case to the exclusion of others. As Wall J said in *Re M* (*Application for Care Order*) [1995] 3 FCR at 633; "any allegation of sexual abuse should be taken seriously, but it must be put in context and assessed calmly, rationally and objectively. Above all it should not be allowed ... to dictate the whole future of the proceedings". That principle should apply to all investigations.

Wall J also said in *Re M*: "it is essential for the investigator not only to proceed with caution, but to establish as early as possible precisely what is being alleged, and above all not to allow the allegation to become embroidered or exaggerated".

A number of questions do have to be asked as a matter of urgency. Is the child in immediate danger? Does the child need to go to hospital? Can the child stay at or return home? Can the person against whom an allegation has been made be assisted or required to leave home in order that the child can remain, pending further investigation? Would placement with relatives be appropriate and safe? Is temporary accommodation under section 20 appropriate and safe? Is an Emergency Protection Order needed? What services could or should be offered? The same questions should be asked in respect of any child who comes to the attention of the authority as a result of their enquiries.

These questions may need to be asked in discussion between agencies, and may need to be the subject of investigation by more than one agency. If so, an inter-agency strategy, as proposed in *Working Together under the Children Act 1989 (HMSO, 1991 at para 5.13)*, should be developed to ensure the proper management of the enquiries. This will need to include decisions about:

i.   who will carry out any necessary interviews of the informant, the carers, any person against whom an allegation has been made, and any other relevant person;

ii.   what arrangements should be put in place for interviewing the child, if necessary;

iii. whether a medical examination to obtain forensic evidence (or for other reasons) is necessary and if so where and when and by whom it should be carried out and when a report will be available;

The method of investigation may need to be considered, so that if there is a possibility of legal proceedings, evidence is obtained which will satisfy the requirements of the court. In *Re M (supra)* Wall J said: "it would be quite wrong for play therapy ever to be used as an investigative tool in an inquiry as to whether or not a child had been sexually abused. Therapy is a form of treatment: treatment necessarily implied a condition which is being treated. Therapy specifically designed to treat a child who has been sexually abused should in my view only occur once it is clearly established that the child has been so abused."

A distinction may nonetheless need to be drawn between the situation described by Wall J and cases where a child is showing symptoms of having suffered a traumatic event, creating the need for treatment of the trauma, during which the child provides evidence of having been harmed.

In *Re M* (*Minors*) [1993] 1 FLR 822 Butler-Sloss LJ said: "It is important to draw distinctions between interviews with young children for the purposes of investigation, assessment and therapy. It would be rare, I would assume, that interviews for a specifically therapeutic purpose would be provided for use in court. Generally it is desirable that interviews with young children should be conducted as soon as possible after the allegations are first raised, should be few in number and should have investigation as their primary purpose. However, an expert interview of a child at a later stage, if conducted in such a way as to satisfy the court that the child has given information after acceptable questioning, may be a valuable part of the evidence for consideration as to whether abuse has occurred. No rigid rules can be laid down and it is for the court to decide whether such evidence is or is not of assistance."

Emergency protection

It may be necessary to consider whether application has to be made for an emergency protection order. Section 44 provides that a court may make an emergency protection order if it is satisfied that "there is reasonable cause to believe that the child is likely to suffer significant harm if (i) he is not removed to accommodation provided by or on behalf of the applicant; or (ii) he does not remain in the place where he is then being accommodated".

This is a test as to future harm, so that if other arrangements can be made for a child, such as a safe placement with relatives, or the parent is willing for the child to be accommodated under section 20, an order may not be necessary. The person thought to be responsible for the likely harm may be prepared to leave the household voluntarily, although enquiries would have to be made as to whether the arrangement can be relied upon. It may be possible to obtain an order under sections 38A or 44A (as added by Schedule 6 of the Family Law Act 1996) in respect of such a person requiring him to leave the house.

Emergencies should be just that and not a routine method of commencing care proceedings. Wall J noted in *Re M*: "unless there is an emergency or grave and immediate danger to a child, precipitate action is unlikely to be in the interests of the child".

Hollings J has given guidance in *Re A (Child Abuse: Guidelines)* [1992] 1 FLR at 444:

"1. Where possible, application should not be made to take children into care ex parte and for the initial purposes of a medical examination unless there is an immediate apprehension of emergency or there are reasonable grounds for believing that the parents would refuse to co-operate in arranging medical examinations.

2. Save in emergencies, case conferences should be held before a child is sought to be removed.

3. Early morning removals of children from their home by police, even though in conjunction with social services, should only be effected when there are clear grounds for believing that significant harm would otherwise be caused to the children or vital evidence is only obtainable by such means."

Considering care proceedings

The threshold criteria are not in themselves grounds or reasons for making a care or supervision order. The Act's philosophy of encouraging work with parents without recourse to court orders has led to a reduction in the need for care proceedings. Initially there was a marked decrease, but the Department of Health published new guidance. The *Children Act Report 1992 (Lord Chancellor's Department at para 2.21)* advised: "Where a local authority determines that control of the child's circumstances is necessary to promote his welfare then compulsory intervention, as part of a carefully planned process, will always be the appropriate remedy. Local authorities should not feel inhibited by the working in partnership provisions of the Children Act from seeking appropriate court orders." ... "Equally, the existence of a court order should not of itself impede a local authority from continuing its efforts at working in partnership with the families of children in need. The two processes are not mutually exclusive. Each has a role to play, often simultaneously, in the case management of a child at risk."

Since publication of the guidance, there has been a gradual upturn in applications, although it levelled off by the end of 1994 and, as shown in the *Final Report of the Children Act Advisory Committee* (*Lord Chancellor's Department, 1997, at Table 1*), has been dropping since, as local authorities have moved their focus away from child protection. It is not clear whether the decreases and increases indicate a proper balance between respecting and promoting the responsibility of parents and promoting the welfare of children.

If the local authority believes that the threshold criteria are satisfied, it should then decide whether to apply for an order or whether it does not need an order because there are other ways of making up the deficit in parenting, for example through the provision of services under Part 3 of the Act, or because the wider family can provide. If reasonable parental care of the child is lacking, so that there has been or is a risk of significant harm to the child, either someone must be shown to supply it or the authority should, through its care plan, ensure adequate care.

Often quoted is the simplistic legal advice allegedly given by local authority solicitors that the court will not make an order if the parent is cooperating. The justification given is the principle of partnership, based on the exercise of shared parental responsibility and the supposed no order provision in section 1(5).

Partnership should assume the exercise of genuine responsibility. Cooperation may be one aspect of partnership, but in itself is insufficient if it is simply masked compliance which disappears when problems arise. Particular care must be taken with parents who have long term and entrenched problems which may exhibit as personality disorder, mental health difficulties or substance abuse.

The comments in *Children Act News*, published by the Department of Health in June 1993 should be noted:

"The notion of partnership, it is said, derives from the provision on parental responsibility, which remains whether or not a care order has been made. The care order gives parental responsibility to the local authority and under section 33(3) the power to curb the parents' use of their responsibility. The issue is therefore not whether further working in partnership is possible, but whether section 1, that the child's welfare is the paramount consideration, is satisfied and whether it would be better for the child for the authority to have parental responsibility under sections 31 and 33."

The following may provide a proper basis for taking care proceedings:

a.   the provision of more extended protection for children;

b.   a framework for facilitating change; and/or

c.   an underpinning for planning the future of children who cannot return home.

In order to inform these purposes, the following questions should be asked:

1.   Do the parents accept that the child has suffered and/or is likely to suffer significant harm and recognise the causes of that harm?

2.   In serious cases of significant harm, can the parents really be expected to exercise parental responsibility appropriately?

3.   Is there real (and continuing) agreement about the plans and can those with parental responsibility be relied on to exercise it consistently?

4.   Will the advantages of taking proceedings outweigh the possible disadvantages for the child, such as the effect on the child and family, especially if rehabilitation is still planned?

5.   Will there be a benefit to the child in establishing by judicial findings that the threshold criteria are satisfied?

Care proceedings

The 'threshold criteria'

Section 31 empowers the court to make a care order or a supervision order, in respect of a child under 17 (or 16 if married), only if the court is satisfied that:

a.   the child concerned is suffering significant harm, or is likely to suffer significant harm; and

b.   the harm or likelihood of harm is attributable to –

  i.   the care given to the child, or likely to be given to him if the order were not made, not being what it would be reasonable to expect a parent to give to him; or

  ii.   the child's being beyond parental control.

Where the facts relate to impairment of health or development, section 31(10) requires the court to compare the health or development with what could reasonably be expected of a similar child.

The conditions have come to be known as the 'threshold criteria', and can conveniently be described as in the chart at Figure 1.

Is the child suffering or likely to suffer harm?

The court must be satisfied that the child is suffering or is likely to suffer harm. The first leg should relate to an existing condition and the second to a prediction. The second was introduced in the Children Act to deal with those cases, previously the cause of many applications in wardship, where there were grave risks to a child, but no evidence of actual harm.

*   *'is suffering'*

The House of Lords has considered the meaning of 'is suffering' in *Re M (A Minor) (Care Order: Threshold Conditions)* [1994] 1 FLR 577. The court had to decide whether it could be satisfied that the child 'is suffering', because there was harm at the time of local authority intervention, if the child had been removed from harm by the time of the hearing. Lord Mackay said: "I would conclude that the natural construction of the conditions in s31(2) is that where, at the time the application is

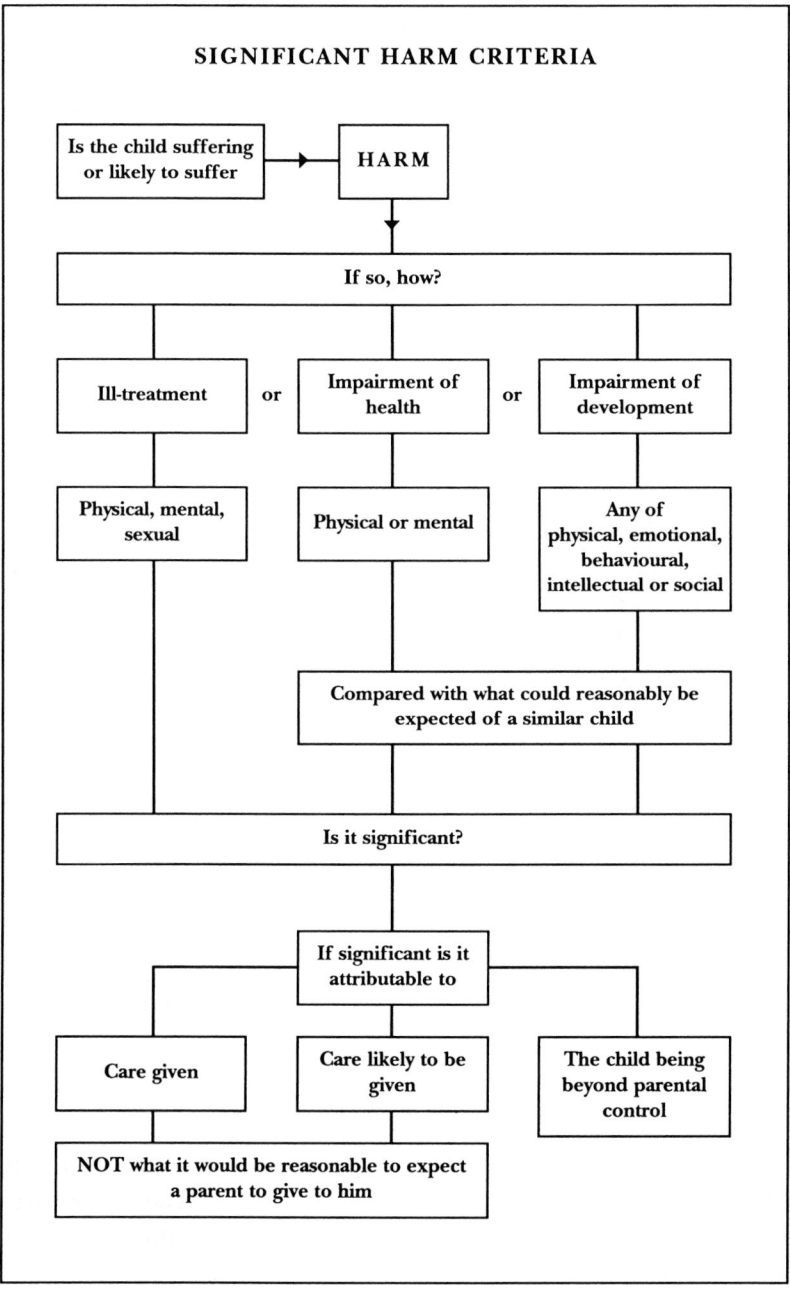

Figure 1

to be disposed of, there are in place arrangements for the protection of the child by the local authority on an interim basis which protection has been continuously in place for some time, the relevant date with respect to which the court must be satisfied is the date at which the local authority initiated the procedure for protection under the Act from which these arrangements follow."

- *'likely to suffer'*

The phrase 'likely to suffer' was introduced with the intention of providing a remedy where harm had not occurred but there were considerable future risks for the child. Such cases arise where the child is in danger from birth, where the parents are mentally ill or drug addicted, where an abuser returns to the household, or where a previous child has died in the household.

'Likely' may be used in different senses and not necessarily on a balance of probabilities or more likely than not. The House of Lords held in *Re H and R (Child Sexual Abuse: Standard of Proof)* [1996] 1 FLR 80 that the word 'likely' was being used in the sense of a real possibility that could not sensibly be ignored having regard to the nature and gravity of the feared harm in the particular case, rather than in the sense of more likely than not.

Problems arise where the likelihood is based on facts that could not be satisfied on the balance of probabilities, such as an allegation of sexual abuse (as in *Re H and R*) or, as in *Re P (Minor) (Care: Evidence)* [1994] 2 FLR 751, where the only evidence of likely harm depended on the death of a previous child in the care of the parents. Since the authority could not prove that the death was non accidental, there was no factual basis for a finding of likelihood of harm to the surviving child.

Is the harm attributable to care given or likely to be given?

The court must be satisfied that the significant harm is attributable to the care given to the child not being what it would be reasonable to expect a parent to give to the child or that the likelihood of harm is attributable to the care likely to be given. Harm caused solely by a third party is therefore excluded, unless the parent has failed to prevent it.

Care of the reasonable parent

The care given or likely to be given must be 'not what it would be reasonable to expect a parent to give the child'. This requires a test to be applied as to whether a hypothetical reasonable parent would provide adequate care, so that parents cannot argue that they have particular problems, that they are feckless, unintelligent, irresponsible, alcoholic, drug abusers, poor or otherwise disadvantaged, which justify them in providing a lower standard of care. Those matters might be relevant to the question of whether an order should be made, if their problems could be ameliorated by the provision of other services by the local authority, but they will not enable them to avoid fulfilling the threshold criteria.

Care of the child in question

The court has to consider the care which should be given to the child in question rather than an average child. If the child has particular difficulties, say in relation to his behaviour or handicap, the court should consider what a reasonable parent would provide for him. This could require a higher or different standard of care than for an average child.

The standard of proof

It should be remembered that the standard of proof in civil proceedings is different to that in criminal proceedings, where guilt must be proved beyond reasonable doubt. In *Re H and R* (*supra*) the House of Lords approved by a majority the following principles for care proceedings: "The standard of proof is the balance of probabilities. The more serious the allegation, the more convincing the evidence needed to tip the balance in respect of it. The difference lies in the cogency of the evidence needed to tip the balance, not in the degree to which the balance needs to be tipped."

To decide an issue the court must identify and, when disputed, decide the relevant facts and then reach a conclusion on the crucial issue. A decision by a court on the likelihood of a future happening must be founded on a basis of present facts and the inferences fairly to be drawn from them.

The threshold was comparatively low but it did require proof of the relevant facts.

Other allegations might suffice to prove a likelihood of future harm, although harm in the past had not been established. Even though no maltreatment was proved, the evidence could establish a combination of profoundly worrying features affecting the care of a child within the family. The Lords considered that there was a range of facts which might satisfy the criteria, including the history of members of a family, the state of relationships within a family, proposed changes within the membership of a family, parental attitudes, and omissions which might not reasonably have been expected, just as much as actual physical assault. They included threats and abnormal behaviour by a child and unsatisfactory parental responses to complaints or allegations and facts which might be minor in isolation but when taken together might suffice to satisfy the court of likely future harm.

Application of the welfare principle to care proceedings

When the court is satisfied of the threshold criteria, it must as a separate matter, decide what order, if any to make. In some cases where there are contentious factual issues there may be a split final hearing as was ordered in *Re S (Care Proceedings: Split Hearing)* [1996] 2 FLR 773. At the first part the court will decide whether the threshold criteria are satisfied. At the second stage the court will decide whether to make a care or supervision order under section 31, an order under section 8 (though not with a care order) or no order.

The court must apply the principles contained in section 1, that the welfare of the child is the paramount consideration, have regard to the fact that delaying a decision is likely to prejudice the welfare of the child, consider the checklist, and not make an order unless it considers that doing so would be better for the child than making no order at all. The local authority's intentions for the child are of the utmost importance, since they justify the making of an order.

In practice the application of the welfare principle means that the court must be satisfied that the outcome of the proceedings provides the best available arrangements, having taken account of the checklist and what would happen if no order were to be made. In order to satisfy the court that it is better for the child to make an order, the authority should be able to indicate what plans will be put into effect as a result of the order. The court must, therefore, consider the care plan of the local authority. The application form for an order under section 31 contains a requirement that the plans of the applicant are set out. It was held in *Manchester City Council v F* [1993] 1 FLR 419 that care plans should follow the headings set out in Volume 3 of the *Department of Health Guidance on Family Placements* (*at para 2.62*), which refers to the *Arrangements for Placement of Children (General) Regulations 1991*.

If the court is not satisfied that the care plan meets the requirement to make the welfare of the child the paramount consideration, or if the facts of the plan are not all known, it may refuse to make a care order. It was recognised, however, in *Re J* (*Minors*) (*Care Plan*) [1994] 1 FLR 253, that the court must strike a balance between being satisfied that the plan is appropriate and avoiding an overzealous investigation into matters which are within the administrative discretion of the local authority.

The Court of Appeal said in *Re P* (*Minors*) (*Interim Order*) [1993] 2 FLR 742 that questions with respect to the upbringing of a child should be determined with regard to the principle that any delay is likely to prejudice the child's welfare. Questions should be determined with finality and as much speed as is consistent with justice and the welfare of the child. Once a question has been determined, the court should seldom, if ever, make continued use of its powers of adjournment under section 38. This was consistent with the policy proposed in Volume 1 of the *Department of Health Guidance on Court Orders* that it was contrary to the scheme and intention of the legislation to make continuous interim care orders, so that the court could keep control over the progress of a case.

On the other hand if the court was awaiting the outcome of an assessment, which might be important to future plans and the appropriate order, the court could be justified in using its range of powers, whether section 8 orders or an interim care order rather than a full care order. 'Planned and purposeful delay', it was suggested in *C v Solihull Metropolitan Borough Council* [1993] 1 FLR 290, could be beneficial to the child.

While the making of an interim care order to control the plans of a local authority is clearly contrary to the intention of the legislation, no other method of ensuring a phased rehabilitation was provided to the courts. The Court of Appeal took the view in *Buckinghamshire County Council v M* [1994] 2 FLR 506, that it must be within the court's power to reach a decision which favoured the return of a child to the parent, against the wishes of the local authority. If return needed to be phased, an interim order might be the only way that the court could ensure that the return remained under control and was open to review by the court.

Section 1(3)(g) of 'the checklist' requires the court to consider the "range of powers available ... in the proceedings in question". Even though the threshold criteria are satisfied the court may, therefore, still decide not to make a care or supervision order. If the criteria are not satisfied, the court still has power to make orders under section 8 of the Act.

Interim orders and directions

Section 32 requires a court hearing an application under Part IV to draw up a timetable with a view to disposing of the application without delay and to give such directions as it considers appropriate for the purpose of ensuring, so far as is reasonably practicable, that the time-table is adhered to. Directions for the conduct of the proceedings are made under rules of court. The court should control the progress of the proceedings by setting a timetable for the submission and service of evidence including experts' reports. Directions appointments are important hearings and not mere formalities. The *Family Proceedings Rules 1991, (rule 4.14)* and the *Family Proceedings Courts (Children Act 1989) Rules 1991 (rule 14)* require the court to consider how the case is being managed. A party must attend, unless the court otherwise directs. It is essential that those attending to represent a party understand the issues in the case. Detailed guidance on case management is given in *Re MD and TD (Minors) (Time Estimates)* [1994] 2 FLR 336 and *Re A and B (No 2)* [1995] 1 FLR 351.

Where, on an application for a care or supervision order, the proceedings are adjourned or where the court in any proceedings gives a direction under section 37 for an authority to investigate the child's circumstances, the court may make an interim care or supervision order under section 38(2), if satisfied that there are reasonable grounds for believing that the threshold criteria are satisfied.

Where the court makes an interim care or supervision order, it may give such directions under section 38(6) as it considers appropriate with regard to medical or psychiatric examination or other assessment of the child and may direct that no examination or assessment is to take place at all or unless the court directs. A direction may be given or varied at any time during the period of an interim order.

The court has jurisdiction to order or prohibit any assessment that involved the participation of the child. It is directed to providing the court with the material that, in the view of the court, was required to enable it to reach a proper decision at the final hearing of the application for a care order. The House of Lords held in *Re C (Interim care order: Residential assessment)* [1997] 1 FLR 1 that although the section referred to the examination or assessment of the child, a child could not be divorced from its environment, so that the direction could include another person. The court could dictate the placement of the child during an interim care order for the purposes of an assessment and could direct the authority to fund any necessary placement, although it would take into account the cost and the fact that local authority resources were limited. It remains the case, as decided in *Re L (A Minor)* [1996] 2 FCR 706, that the court may not order that a child live with its parent during the course of an interim care order, since that is a discretion vested in the local authority. Nor can the court direct the provision of services: *Re J (A Minor) (Specific Issue Order: Leave to Apply)* [1995] 1 FLR 669.

The effects of a care order

Section 33 provides that under a care order a local authority is required to receive the child and keep him in their care while the order is in force. The authority acquires parental responsibility, but the parent does not cease to have parental responsibility solely because some other person acquires it. A person with parental responsibility is not entitled to act in a way which would be incompatible with any order made under the Act, so that a parent is not entitled to exercise parental responsibility in contravention of the care order. Specifically the authority has the power to determine the extent to which a parent or guardian may meet his parental responsibility insofar as it is necessary to do so to safeguard or promote the child's welfare.

Evidence in care proceedings

Statements will be made in care proceedings which will be a mixture of fact and opinion evidence, both as to the threshold criteria and on the application of the welfare principle.[1] The welfare checklist provides a useful focus for evidence, since it includes elements of the threshold criteria. The checklist in section 1(3) requires consideration of:

a. the ascertainable wishes and feelings of the child concerned, in the light of age and understanding;

b. his physical, emotional and educational needs;

c. the likely effect of any change of circumstances;

d. his age, sex, background and any other relevant characteristics, which include religious persuasion, racial origin and cultural and linguistic background;

e. any harm which he has suffered or is at risk of suffering;

f. how capable each of his parents, and any other relevant person, is of meeting his needs.

Additional evidence might be acquired from statements by an alleged abuser, carers, others associated with the child or the child him or herself. In considering harm attention should be paid to physical indicators, such as height and weight charts and X-rays and material expounded by other authors in this book.

Evidence of this kind may in part need to be given by an expert witness, a person who has undergone a course of special study or experience as will render him expert in a particular subject. It is for the judge to decide whether the person is suitably skilled. The Children Act Advisory Committee advise that all experts should have certain basic skills, which are set out in a core CV in the 1993/4 report.[2]

Evidence from the child

In some cases, usually those where allegations of sexual abuse have been made, the main source of information may well be the child. Children are not necessarily regarded as less reliable than adults, although the courts will still exercise caution. Reliance solely on children's evidence can present problems of credibility, suggestibility, retraction and confusion of events and detail, especially where there have been delays.

Hearsay evidence may be given in accordance with the Children (Admissibility of Hearsay Evidence) Order 1993. This may be given on videotape. The court's approach in civil proceedings was considered by Butler-Sloss LJ in *Re W (Minors) (Wardship: Evidence)* [1990] 1 FLR 203. "In wardship, therefore, the rules as to the reception of statements made by children to others, whether doctors, police officers, social workers, welfare officers, foster-mothers, school teachers or others, may be relaxed and the information may be received by the judge. He has a duty to look at it and consider what weight, if any, he should give to it. The weight which he places upon the information is a matter for the exercise of his discretion. He may totally disregard it. He may wish to rely upon some or all of it." ... "Allegations of sexual abuse made in a statement by a child naming a perpetrator presented considerable problems and would, unsupported, rarely be sufficiently cogent and reliable for a court to be satisfied on the balance of probabilities that the person named was the perpetrator. The evidence may, however, reveal a clear indication that the child has been exposed to inappropriate sexual activities and may be sufficiently compelling to satisfy the judge that the child has been subject to serious sexual abuse. Statements of a child may well be supported by the manner in which the child gives the description and in other aspects of his or her behaviour. The giving of the statement is unlikely to be neutral in the inferences to be drawn."

Evidence of this nature may well be given on videotape. Ward LJ made the following observations about videorecorded evidence in *Re N (A Minor) (Child Abuse: Evidence)* [1996] 2 FLR 214:

"1.   The recording was admitted as a form of hearsay evidence. It was for the judge to decide its weight and credibility. He would judge the internal consistency and inconsistency of the story. He would look for any inherent improbabilities in the truth of what the child related and would decide what part, if any, he could believe.

2.   The judge would receive expert evidence to explain and interpret the video. This would cover such things as the nuances of emotion and behaviour, the gestures and the body movements, the use or non-use of language and its imagery, the vocal inflections and intonations, the pace and pressure of the interview, the child's intellectual and verbal abilities, or lack of them, and any signs or the absence of signs of fantasising.

3.   It was for the judge to separate admissible from inadmissible expert evidence. Proper evidence from an expert would be couched in terms that a particular fact was consistent or inconsistent with sexual abuse, and that it rendered the child's evidence capable or incapable of being accepted by the judge as true.

4.   Evidence of a diagnosis of sexual abuse called for a very high level of expertise. For the court to rely on opinion evidence, even to admit it, the qualification of the witness must extend beyond experience gained as a social worker and require clinical experience as or akin to a child psychologist or child psychiatrist."

Subsequent to that decision, Butler-Sloss LJ has held in *Re M and R (Child Abuse: Evidence)* [1996] 2 FLR 195 that an expert's evidence as to a witness's credibility is admissible. Nevertheless the court retains a discretion not to admit such evidence and questions as to weight and relevance are matters for the judge. As Wall J held in *Re B (Care Proceedings: Case conduct)* [1998] Times, May 13, evidence of propensity or assessment of a party should be on the basis of facts found by the court, if they are in dispute.

The use of expert witnesses

If the evidence to be given requires the child to be medically or psychiatrically examined or otherwise assessed, the leave of the court or the justices' clerk must be obtained. Court rules provide that no evidence arising out of an examination may be adduced without the consent of the court. Any documents held by the court may only be disclosed to a person not involved in the proceedings with the consent of the court. By these means the court can control the input of expert evidence and will want to know what a particular expert can contribute to the case. Courts will give greater weight to the evidence of an expert who has seen the child, but may in certain circumstances grant leave only for disclosure of the papers.

The decisions of the courts in relation to experts all confirm the trend towards limiting expert evidence to those cases where expert evidence is required for any particular issue. This is highlighted by the *Practice Direction on the subject of case management* [1995] 1 FLR 456 issued by the President of the Family Division on 31 January 1995 providing *inter alia* that:

The parties and their legal advisers must also use their best endeavours:

a. to confine the issues of the evidence called to what is reasonably considered to be essential for the proper presentation of their case;

b. to reduce or eliminate issues for expert evidence;

c. in advance of the main hearing to agree which are the issues or main issues.

Instruction of experts

In *Re C (Expert Evidence: Disclosure: Practice)* [1995] 1 FLR 204 Cazalet J directed:

"Generalised orders for leave to disclose papers to an expert should never be made. The area of expertise, the issues to be addressed, and the particular expert should be identified in advance of appointment, thereby facilitating a timetable for the preparation of the report, the date for filing it with the court, and the availability of the expert to give evidence if required. If that is done, only in the most exceptional cases will it be necessary for there to be extensions of time. Advocates who seek such leave have a positive duty to place all relevant information before the court at the earliest opportunity and the court has a positive duty to inquire into that information, and, in particular, the category of expert evidence sought to be adduced, the name and availability of the expert, the relevance to the issues in the case, whether the evidence can properly be obtained by the joint instruction of one expert by the parties, and whether expert evidence may properly be adduced by one party only, for example the guardian ad litem."

Medical experts asked to give reports must be fully instructed; the letter of instruction should set out the context in which the opinion is sought and define specific questions for the expert to address. The letter should identify any relevant issues of fact to enable each expert to give an opinion on each set of competing issues, so that the court upon determining the facts can consider the relevant expert opinion.

The letter of instruction should list the documents to be sent to the expert, and careful thought should be given to the selection of relevant and necessary documentation. In order to assist the expert, an agreed chronology and background history should be provided as part of the core bundle. An expert should never be provided with an unsorted pile of papers.

The letter of instruction should always be disclosed to other parties, who should be invited to contribute to defining the appropriate issues, the relevant documentation, the history, and questions to be addressed. The resulting letter must be included in the bundle of documents for use in the court. Experts should not hesitate to seek further information and documentation when required. Such requests should form part of the core bundle.

Doctors who have clinical experience of a child prior to the commencement of proceedings should have all clinical material made available for inspection by the court and other experts – for example medical notes, hospital records, X-rays, photographs, and correspondence.

Cazalet J also suggested in *Re C* that it should be a condition of appointment of any expert that he be required to hold discussions with other experts instructed in the same field of expertise in advance of the hearing in order to identify areas of agreement and dispute, which should be incorporated into a schedule for the court.

Experts who are to give evidence must be kept up to date with developments in the case, relevant to their opinions, and it is the duty of the solicitor instructing the expert to provide such information. It is the duty of the advocate calling an expert to ensure that the witness in advance of giving evidence has seen all fresh relevant material and is aware of new developments, so that the expert can consider the effect upon opinions previously expressed.[3]

In *Re AB* (*Child Abuse: Expert Witnesses*) [1995] 1 FL R 181 Wall J set out the duties and responsibilities of experts in child cases.

"1. Expert evidence presented to the court should be and should be seen to be the independent product of the expert uninfluenced as to form or content by the exigencies of litigation.

2. An expert witness should provide independent assistance to the court by way of objective unbiased opinion in relation to matters within his expertise. An expert witness in the High Court should never assume the role of advocate.

3. An expert witness should state the facts or assumptions on which his opinion is based. He should not omit to consider material facts which detract from his concluded opinion.

4. An expert witness should make it clear when a particular question falls outside his expertise.

5. If an expert's opinion is not properly researched because he considers that insufficient data is available then this must be stated with an indication that the opinion is no more than a provisional one.

6. If, after exchange of reports, an expert witness changes his view on a material matter, such change of view should be communicated ... to the other side without delay and when appropriate to the court."

Summary

It can be seen that certain types of children's cases will best be managed by the local authority through the initiation of care proceedings. To ensure that the case is properly conducted in the interests of the child, it is essential that social workers and the local authorities legal representatives undertake good preparatory work. In accordance with matters discussed earlier, this will require analysis of the issues, adequate investigation, assessment of facts and opinions by appropriate professionals and consideration of how that material can best be presented for the court. These matters must all be considered in the light of statutory provisions, case law interpretation, departmental guidance, local procedures and the best practice of each professional involved.

References

1. On the preparation of documents for court see *Reporting to Court under the Children Act: A Handbook for Social Services,* Plotnikoff and Woolfson, (HMSO,1996) and *Child Psychiatry and the Law* (Gaskell, 3rd ed., forthcoming).

2. See also the *Best Practice Handbook* (Lord Chancellor's Department, 1997) and the *Expert Witness Pack* (Family Law, 1997).

3. For further discussion of expert evidence in child care cases see *Rooted Sorrows* (Family Law, 1997).

CHAPTER TWO:

Significant harm: implications for Local Authorities

Margaret Adcock

Working with the concept of significant harm requires an understanding of the policy and practice developments envisaged in the Children Act 1989, the way the Act has been implemented by agencies, and the subsequent changes in policy and practice advocated by the Government.

At present there seems to be a wide variation amongst local authorities in the way significant harm is understood and defined. There is no clear agreement about the nature or level of harm deemed *significant* or about what is *significant enough* to warrant local authority intervention or to warrant removal of the child. Some professionals do not define what is happening to the child as significant harm or likely significant harm until they think there are grounds for care proceedings which will then be commenced. In other places there are differing views about whether the existence or the likelihood of what is agreed to be significant harm necessarily means that the child protection system should be used at all. In some cases it has been thought unnecessary to use the legislation to protect children and there have been tragic consequences. Elsewhere it appears that the child protection system is still the gateway to resources for families without much consideration about whether the process is necessary or beneficial for families.

Even when significant harm has been formally identified there seem to be variations in the way in which it is managed. Thoburn, Brandon and Lewis (*1997*) found that in a sample of children where significant harm was identified, some cases were conferenced but not registered, others were registered and a few resulted in care proceedings. Decisions about the management of a case were usually related to whether it seemed possible to deal with the significant harm without registration or care proceedings.

Overall it seems that there is a clear need to consider what events and processes harm children significantly and to establish a *professional* definition of significant harm, based on knowledge of child development, to co-exist with the legal definition. This definition can then provide a framework for both the management of significant harm and the development of preventive and treatment services. It will involve considering also the needs of both children and parents, what helps people to change and what part the use of partnership, authority, and compulsion might play in the process.

Professional definitions of significant harm

There needs to be a multi-professional definition of what constitutes significant harm, which co-exists with the legal definition. This definition should provide a basis for professional diagnosis, intervention and management and assist professionals in deciding whether to provide services under section 17 or to take care proceedings. It would need, as Graham et al (*1985*) have suggested, to be able to link advances in the understanding of child development and the outcomes of abuse to public and political judgements about acceptable standards of child care. It must take account of work that has already been done on race, culture, disability and gender.

The establishment of such a definition would be particularly useful for workers in social services, since their decision-making is often perceived as bureaucratically rather than clinically based. Parker (*1986*) commented "Social workers are not involved in the day to day care of children. They do not have that as a constant point of reference for the success of what they are doing; general criteria have to serve instead. Just as the profession of child care was largely created by Government action after the last war, so the changing emphases and priorities in policy and legislation have provided the yardstick against which social work in child care has come to judge its performance. It is not surprising, therefore, that these criteria may sometimes distort the decisions that have to be made."

A professional diagnosis of significant harm, or likely significant harm, does not necessarily mean that the child has a need for immediate protection by removal from home. It means that the child and family need help or services to prevent the child's development being further impaired. The advantage of a professional as opposed to a court-imposed diagnosis is that it can be made at an early stage before a legal standard of proof has necessarily been reached. Early interventions may mean that harmful outcomes can be prevented. Children who are judged professionally to be suffering, or likely to suffer significant harm, may be assisted by services at home, in the first instance. They may then be removed from home at a later stage if change does not occur. In many cases this could be carefully planned and might give more opportunity for finding the appropriate resources and placements for the child away from home.

Significant harm needs to be understood separately from child abuse or neglect, although the two may co-exist. The two can be differentiated by the idea that child abuse describes *acts* and *omissions,* significant harm describes *effects.* The definition of harm in the Act is ill treatment or the impairment of health and development. Ill treatment may lead to the impairment or likely impairment of health and development. Impairment may also occur without ill treatment to the child as a result, for example, of living in a home where there is violence between the adults. Some children may need protection to prevent the recurrence of ill treatment; any child whose health or development has been impaired may need services to deal with the consequences of this. Parents may need services to help them not to ill treat their child nor to further impair the child's health or development, and to facilitate them in helping the child to recover from what has happened.

Bentovim (*Chapter 3*) has provided a definition of significant harm which would form a useful professional baseline. He defines harm in terms of its effects on a child's development. He states: *"Significant harm may be thought of as a compilation of significant events, both acute and long-standing, which interact with the child's ongoing development, and interrupt, alter or impair physical and psychological development. Being the victim of significant harm is likely to have a profound effect on a child's view of themselves as a person and on their future lives. Significant harm represents a major symptom of failure of adaptation by parents to their role, and also involves both the family and society."*

The significance of harm

The *significance* of harm may therefore be largely in its long-term effects on the child's development and there is now quite a considerable body of research, mainly from the USA, to show this (*Skuse and Bentovim, 1996*).

Crittenden and Claussen (*1993*) suggest that critical factors that will determine the outcome, i.e. the significance of the harm to the child are:-

- The chronicity of the maltreatment.

- The degree of distortion of the child's self-perception.

- Limited access to developmentally normative and growth-producing experiences.

All these factors are likely to have a harmful effect on the child's development.

Bentovim suggests in Chapter 3 that development can be conceived as comprising a number of age and stage-relevant tasks. The way in which these are achieved has the potential to affect future outcome in the direction of good or less good states of adjustment. Successful resolution of early stage-salient issues increases the possibility of subsequent successful adjustment and vice versa. Widom (*1966*) described the compounding effects of a negative process in the following way: "Deficits or dysfunctional behaviours at one developmental period will lay the groundwork for subsequent dysfunctional behaviours. Deficits manifest at one age continue to exert an influence at the next stage unless an intervention occurs. For example, malnutrition in infancy in the neurological or medical domain may lead to impaired intellectual or cognitive functioning in toddlers which in turn may affect IQ and in turn affect school performance in a negative way and in turn lead to impaired performance as an adult."

It may, however, be possible to prevent negative outcomes by appropriate interventions, as Figure 1 devised by Widom (*in press*) shows. It is as

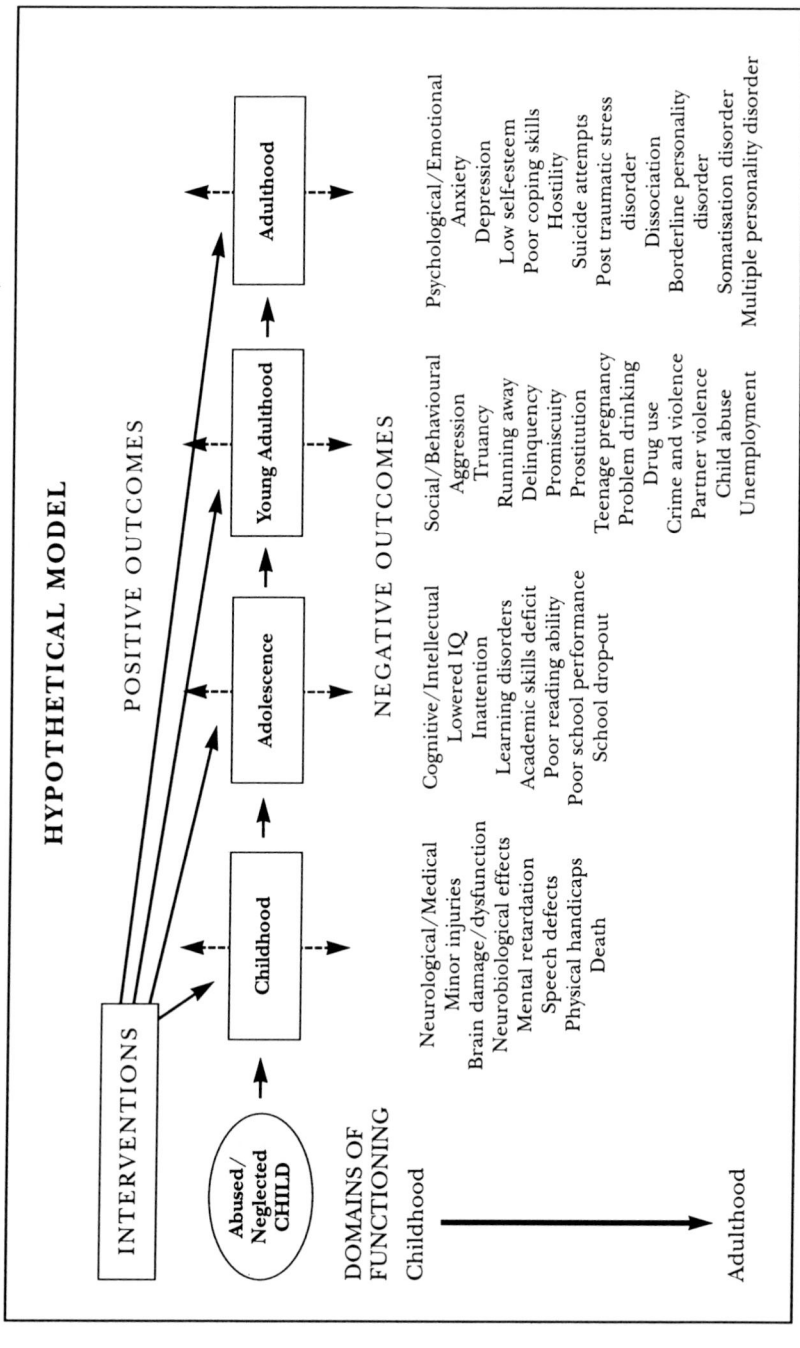

HYPOTHETICAL MODEL

POSITIVE OUTCOMES

NEGATIVE OUTCOMES

INTERVENTIONS

Abused/ Neglected CHILD

| Childhood | Adolescence | Young Adulthood | Adulthood |

DOMAINS OF FUNCTIONING

Childhood

Neurological/Medical
Minor injuries
Brain damage/dysfunction
Neurobiological effects
Mental retardation
Speech defects
Physical handicaps
Death

Cognitive/Intellectual
Lowered IQ
Inattention
Learning disorders
Academic skills deficit
Poor reading ability
Poor school performance
School drop-out

Social/Behavioural
Aggression
Truancy
Running away
Delinquency
Promiscuity
Prostitution
Teenage pregnancy
Problem drinking
Drug use
Crime and violence
Partner violence
Child abuse
Unemployment

Psychological/Emotional
Anxiety
Depression
Low self-esteem
Poor coping skills
Hostility
Suicide attempts
Post traumatic stress disorder
Dissociation
Borderline personality disorder
Somatisation disorder
Multiple personality disorder

Adulthood

Figure 1

Widom

37

important to offer interventions, and at as early a stage in the child's development as possible, as it is to prevent recurrence of any ill treatment. Interventions would need to be based on assessments and these would need to be based on an understanding of developmental issues. If there are no interventions, the child's development may continue to be adversely affected even though there is no further maltreatment. Studies on resilience make it clear that individuals are affected differently by similar experiences but that previous vulnerabilities may make it harder to cope with subsequent difficulties (*Rutter, 1985*).

The management of significant harm

In managing significant harm the following issues are likely to arise in work with individual families:

- Does the child need protection and removal from the parent.
  What will the consequences be for the child if this action is not taken?

- What does an assessment of both the child and family show?
  Is the child being ill-treated or her/his health and development being impaired? What needs do the child and family have?

- What changes are required to deal with existing difficulties and to ensure that the child's needs are adequately met in the future and her/his health and development is promoted?

- Should services be provided under Section 17 or Section 31?

Local authorities planning services will also need to ask:

- Which children and families are likely to be most in need of services?

- Which services are likely to be most effective in helping parents and children to change?

- Who is most likely to benefit from which services?

- How long should a service be provided?

Answers to these questions are likely to be part knowledge-based, part value-based and part finance-led.

The need for a risk assessment and immediate protection

After a referral most children will remain in their families or extended families at least for a period of time and will be helped on a voluntary basis. However, some children cannot be protected and some families may not be able to change unless there is a degree of compulsion. In some situations there may be a risk of serious harm if immediate action is not taken to separate the child from the abusing parent.

When a referral suggests either that:

— serious ill treatment or impairment of health and development has already occurred, (*see Chapter 3 by Bentovim*) and/or

— one or both parent's capacity to care is seriously impaired because of a history of previous violence, drug or alcohol abuse, mental illness or conduct disorder (*see Chapter 4 by Jones*)

— there is no adequate explanation for what has happened, and/or

— neither parent takes responsibility

there is a real question about the child's safety and the risk of future harm. It may not be possible to protect the child in such circumstances and the child's safety is likely to be best ensured by the alleged abuser leaving or by placing the child elsewhere in a safe situation until a detailed assessment can be undertaken of the whole family.

Farmer and Owen (*1995*) found that the most important element in protection was the physical separation from the abusing parent. In their study 70% of children had been protected twenty months later from further abuse and neglect. They said "Of the children who were effectively protected, this was achieved by total separation from the abusing parent in almost half the cases, while in over a quarter of the cases the children had been separated from the parent who had abused them for part of the follow up period. It is a sobering finding that only about a quarter of the children who had been effectively protected had achieved this safety while living continuously with the parent who was alleged to have abused them."

In situations where the child's removal is proposed, and the parents agree to accommodation, thus obviating the need for an emergency protection order, consideration should still be given to the question of commencing care proceedings. (*See also White, Chapter 1 p16.*) *The Department of Health Study on Court Orders* (*1992*) observed that "voluntary arrangements may be effective in the short term in protecting the child but as the heat of the crisis cools the local authority is left without power to ensure that changes that are necessary *do* take place and that changes that are dangerous do not take place".

If it is decided not to use legal proceedings, it is still important to pay attention to protection issues. Farmer and Owen (*1995*) found that the plans made at initial child protection case conferences set a framework for subsequent practice in relation to both protection issues and to subsequent interventions. This framework was particularly likely to have a continuing positive influence when the key worker was new to the case at the time of the initial conference and when the recommendations were specific, feasible and tailored to the *protection and treatment* issues of the particular child and family.

Assessment

Good assessments will be essential as a basis for deciding what are the concerns for the child and the family, what needs to change and which services and interventions are needed to achieve this. There will need to be very specific and focused assessments of the child. This will help to counteract the tendency to concentrate only on the parents and will also provide information to enable professionals as well as parents to understand more about the child. An assessment of a child needs to be part of the investigation, enquiries and assessment process described by White in Chapter 1. In order to involve families and utilise their strengths and in order to consider needs as well as risks the following issues need to be considered:

- the concerns of the referrers and of the parents;

- any problems or difficulties reported by parents, including history and date of onset;

- the child's perceptions of events and of any problems identified by others;

- parental capacity and the quality of the current care provided by the parent/s;

The assessment should also consider the dimensions recommended in the *Looking after Children Materials* (*HMSO, 1995*) which many local authorities are already using for assessments of children in need:

- Health, including growth and development;

- Education;

- Family and social relationships;

- Social presentation;

- Emotional development and behaviour;

- Self care skills.

Finally there will need to be a detailed analysis of any harm or likely harm (either ill treatment or impairment of health or development) including its nature, history, explanations and consequences. Overall, as recommended in the Department of Health *Protecting Children A Guide to Comprehensive Assessment* (*1988*), assessments should take account of previous life events as well as any immediate need for protection. Emphasis should be placed, as *Messages from Research* (*1995*) suggested, on looking at what has actually happened and is happening to the child and understanding this within the overall context of child development, parental behaviour, family life and the support and risks present in the family's environment. There will need to be a very careful examination of children who are being chronically abused, or neglected, or living with domestic violence, and/or being subjected to emotional abuse. In some cases there may be a need for immediate protection but in most cases intervention should follow a careful assessment of the child's problems and of the family's strengths and difficulties in meeting the child's needs.

Which services are likely to be most effective in helping children and parents to change?

It is important that the interventions offered are specific and are tailored to the needs of the child and family. They need to be based on the assessment of what changes are needed and how they can be brought about. Gough (*1993*), reviewing the research on intervention, warned that, "a broad sweep strategy to psychological interventions is unlikely to produce the results sufficient to convince the policy makers of further investment in these programmes."

If consideration is given first to the information obtained from an assessment of the child along the dimensions already described, it may then be easier to consider, in the light of the child's needs, what services, if any, it would be appropriate to offer to different family members. Services may therefore be needed to address needs arising from:

- Physical, developmental, emotional, behavioural, educational or anti-social problems in the child;

- Family or parent child relationships;

- Parental difficulties in providing appropriate care for the child. These may result from physical or mental ill health, substance abuse, problems with anger management, domestic violence, a history of abuse as a child, marital problems, racial harassment, financial, housing or other problems;

- The child's need for protection.

A multi-disciplinary group would be best able to identify where help is needed and to consider who will provide it. Some problems may be relatively easy to address, if for example they relate to health issues but others may be more difficult. We have to accept that it is not always clear how some adult problems are best dealt with and whether others can, in the present state of our knowledge or the resources available, be resolved within a time scale that also makes it possible to meet children's needs. Not enough is yet known, for example, about really effective methods of dealing with emotional abuse, neglect or domestic violence.

Current research (*Farmer and Owen, 1995*) suggests that a therapeutic relationship with a helping professional may be a key factor in enabling change to occur. This has implications for agencies in allocating workers and ensuring that they can remain with the family over the period of time required for change to take place.

Cicchetti and Toth (*1995*) state also that a developmentally based, empirically validated therapeutic approach to addressing the sequelae of child maltreatment has not yet evolved and that the field is far from a consensus regarding the most effective approach. The range of suggested treatments may reflect the very real heterogeneity of functioning manifested by maltreated children. They suggest the following points need to be considered in planning interventions:

- The child does not exist in isolation but is affected by the home, the school and the broader community;

- The current care, i.e. by the maltreating family or alternative carers, is likely to affect the child's response to treatment;

- Whether the child has ever experienced a positive relationship and, if so, with whom, will also affect whether the child will be able to form a therapeutic alliance with anyone;

They also draw attention to the view of James (*1989*) that:

- Treatment should be developmentally sequenced because "past traumatic events will have a different or additional meaning to the child as he matures, which can impair the progress of development".

All agencies involved with the child should know the conclusions of an assessment so that their own provision for the child can be planned accordingly. Links between those providing services, for example social workers, health visitors, GPs, probation officers, family centres, playgroups, and schools will be particularly important to ensure a unified approach.

How do families change

Partnership, authority and compulsion

It is clear that there must be an integrated approach to family support and child protection to enable professionals to decide if and when there is a need for protection and/or compulsion. All workers need to know how to assess significant harm clinically and offer services but they also have to be able to recognise when the child has a need for protection, either because it is clear that services have not assisted the parents to provide adequate care or because there is a risk of immediate danger. This has implications for the way in which social workers work with families. It means that they have to be able to explain the meaning and use of terms like *partnership, protection, authority* and *compulsion* to families in a way that they can understand. Explanations will need to be understood by people from different races, cultures and religions.

The meaning of partnership

Since the Children Act 1989 there has been great emphasis on the principle of working in partnership but there has also been much debate about what this means and whether it is only possible in voluntary situations. It is clearly important for the successful working of the Act that there is a more detailed understanding shared by families and professionals of what is meant by partnership. Without this children or parents cannot be offered appropriate safeguards and social workers and members of other disciplines will not be able to resolve their dual responsibilities for supporting families and protecting children from harm.

The idea of partnership derives from the concept of parental responsibility which replaces parental rights and duties. Lord Mackay, the Lord Chancellor, said in introducing the Children Bill in the House of Lords, that the term *parental responsibility* was designed to emphasise that the days when a child should be regarded as the possession of his parents were now buried forever. He said that the overriding purpose of parenthood was the responsibility of caring for and raising the child to be a properly developed adult, both physically and morally.

The parent has responsibility by virtue of section 2 of the Act. No other person, including the local authority, has responsibility for the child or authority to exercise any power over the child without consent of the parent or a legal mandate, for example under a care or residence order. Anyone offering services to the family must therefore work in conjunction with the parents. Where a child has sufficient understanding to participate, s/he should also be involved.

Partnership was first described, but not defined, in the 1991 *Department of Health Guidance (Vol 3. para 2.10)*. The Guidance stressed the need for partnership with parents and consultation with children as a guiding principle for the provision of services. Working in partnership is not necessarily synonymous with working with families on a voluntary basis. It also applies where there is a care order. Ways of achieving this have been developed by some social workers and are described in the research on child protection undertaken by both Farmer and Owen (*1995*) and Thoburn et al. (*1995*).

A dictionary definition of partnership is "state of being a partner, sharing, joint business". In the *Department of Health Guidance* partnership is perceived in relation to child-centred goals. It is not an open-ended arrangement. It should be built on a plan arising from an assessment of the child's needs. This is the 'joint business' of partnership. It will be very important that the principle of working in partnership does not become an end in itself, but is always related to the needs of the child. Child-centred partnership is an appropriate feature of services which are directed at promoting the healthy development of children. Understanding the implications of a child's racial or cultural needs or a disability, weighing up alternatives, balancing different kinds of harm and deciding what is the least detrimental alternative for the child imposes further requirements.

The *Department of Health Practice Guide (1995) The Challenge of Partnership in Child Protection* provided useful descriptions of some characteristics of partnership. It stated that:

- The opportunity for families to influence events is an essential part of participation and partnership;

- If children and adults are to influence effectively what happens to their lives, they must be fully informed. They need to know on what matters there can be negotiation;

- Professionals undermine their working relationship with families if they are unclear or equivocal about the extent to which options are available. Families may express a preference for a particular type of service which is not available and it is important that workers are honest about the limitations of services;

- Professionals must be explicit about any new or changed expectations which they have about the care of the child and they must be equally clear with adults and young people about any adjustments to the services provided for the family.

Thoburn (1995) has defined the elements of partnership as *information, consultation and involvement in planning and decision-making*. Howe (1992) provides useful guidance in developing a more detailed understanding of the meaning of partnership and how it is related to other terms such as *helpfulness, empowerment* and *parental control*.

Howe distinguishes initially between voluntary and involuntary clients; those who have a problem may become clients voluntarily, those who *are* a problem become clients whether they like it or not. Parental participation may occur in both voluntary and involuntary situations but will take different forms. In the involuntary situation Howe describes a *play fair* approach. Although the client has not requested involvement with the social worker, the practitioner wishes to be open and clear about all legal, material, and interpersonal aspects of the case. The client should know where s/he is and how s/he stands in the scheme of things. By contrast when the client voluntarily seeks help, the social worker is keen to involve him or her in defining the problem and deciding a course of action. Although the worker and client possess different skills, they are active and equal partners in the relationship.

Howe then distinguishes further between two different types of partnership in practice;

- *Political participation* rests on ideas of social justice. "Clients should know what is happening in matters which affect their lives. They should be kept informed, be aware of resources, consulted about practicalities, and be present and involved when decisions are being made about their children and families."

- *Therapeutic participation* derives from a psychological base, including certain traditions in counselling and social casework, of encouraging full and active participation of the client. It is believed that treatment is more likely to be effective when people are involved in trying to understand their own problems and the solutions to them. The client's participation is not just a matter of promoting rights but also of ensuring that he or she remains in control of his or her experience. Theoretically, all aspects of the worker/client encounter might remain under the client's control.

In child protection cases, however, because of the local authority's duty to investigate under section 47, the parent is, at least temporarily, an involuntary client. Moreover the child is also a client and there is therefore a potential conflict of interests. The type of therapeutic participation described by Howe is limited by the fact that social workers have to make decisions about a child's safety. Howe says "in such cases therapeutic participation would be either insincere, limited, compromised or dangerous ... involuntary clients can only participate on a political and not a therapeutic basis."

Howe then suggests that an appropriate therapeutic basis for participation in child protection work might be one that credits the trained social worker with knowledge and skills about human behaviour which helps them determine what should be done. The professionals, however, can share their knowledge, explain what is happening and discuss the benefits or any disadvantages of any proposed changes. The professional remains the expert but believes that the client should be involved and informed. This involvement should assist and improve the possibility of change.

The use of authority and the relationship between compulsion and change

Authority may be derived from professional expertise but also from statutory power. "All professionals need to be comfortable with and able to use authority appropriately" in order to be able to help families to change and to protect children (*Working Together, 1991*). The evidence from research (*Sainsbury, 1975*) suggests that families can understand and accept the need for statutory authority if it is exercised in an open and honest way.

Rooney (*1988*) states that the better informed the client is concerning what will occur during treatment and what the client should be doing for his or her part of the process, the more likely the client is to derive benefit from the process. He says the worker has three tasks when preparing to work on an involuntary basis: (1) identify non-negotiable requirements from legally involuntary clients, (2) identify negotiable options and free choices, (3) monitor his/her feelings about the alleged offence. Supervisors also need to be involved in this preparation.

The use of statutory authority will involve some degree of compulsion and this may lead to change. An example of this is given by Kagan and Schlosberg (*1989*). They suggest that in some situations a strong child protective service presence can create anxiety in a family which will then lead to change. Some families may be more able to change if the professional who is directly attempting to induce the change does not hold the statutory authority. This professional could be another member of the case manager's team or from a different team or another agency. It may be particularly important for this family worker not to be responsible for the planning, decision-making or direct work with the children. The family worker can stress his/her comparative powerlessness in the decision-making about the children and may then better be able to help parents take some responsibility for choices about what outcomes they would like and how these can be achieved. The family worker can then nurture and support the needy parent(s) in making the change. Kagan and Schlosberg suggest that this is helpful for families who are in perpetual crisis, have very low esteem and have no trust in professional helpers. It is essential however, that everyone working in this situation shares the same values and long terms goals and makes this clear to the family. Without this, the family conflicts are likely to be replayed in the professional group (*Dale et al, 1986*).

It will be necessary for multi-disciplinary groups undertaking this work to try and achieve agreement in advance about how to proceed in both voluntary and involuntary situations, to consider what framework is necessary for this and who will do what. Conferences are critical times for co-ordinating work and recognising the role of each practitioner with the family.

Morrison (*1991*) said: "The relationship between compulsion and change is a complex one, involving both professional and political issues. At its most simple, it is clear that compulsion alone does not lead to change, except in the most concrete and external of ways. But compulsion is not necessarily an enemy of change. To understand the relationship between compulsion and change requires a wider exploration of what motivates people to change and how people change."

In Chapter 5 Morrison describes in some detail a comprehensive model produced by Protchaska and DiClemente (*1986*) which draws out the core components of the change process. This model seems particularly relevant to working with significant harm. (*See diagram p137.*)

Pre-Contemplation

At this stage, many families are at the point where agencies are deciding how to respond to incidents that suggest significant harm has already occurred. Families are often defensive and reluctant to look at the real issues. The motivation for change is often far greater in the agencies than in the family. Assessing the family's ability to move to the contemplation and action stages will be an important factor in judging whether there is a need for a court order.

Contemplation

Assisting families with deeply entrenched patterns of dysfunctional behaviour to make a serious commitment to change requires considerable skill, patience and effort. The crisis-ridden nature of some families means that one is often dealing with a moving target. Simply gaining sufficient stability to assess and catalyse the family's motivation can require the use of statutory intervention. This in itself may act as a powerful external message that things must change. The clearer the family is as to what needs to change and why, and the costs and benefits of change, the better the chance that it will stay in treatment. For some families a court order will be a necessary external sanction to reduce the chance of drop out.

Action

Research on treatment has shown the importance of targeting specific treatments for specific problems and in an ordered sequence where there are multiple issues. Treatment is also much more effective where concrete and visible outcomes are agreed. Thus in contrast to the Contemplation Stage, with work on self evaluation, general ventilation of feelings and specifying problems, this stage will be more action-orientated. Examples might include behavioural or child management problems, or marital work.

Maintenance

By this stage the emphasis is on the consolidation of changes. The family needs to know and accept the dangers of problems re-emerging, and be willing to seek help to prevent relapse. Stability and support will be essential to sustaining change, especially with many families who have such poor experience of problem-solving.

Relapse

This cyclical model of change allows for the reality that few people succeed first time round. Change comes from repeated efforts, re-evaluation, renewing of commitment, and incremental success. Relapse is thus part of, rather than necessarily hostile to, change. Change is a battle between the powerful forces that press us to stay the same and our wish to be different. Court orders in some cases will be crucial in monitoring plans to protect the child.

Should services be offered under section 17 or section 31

The issue is not merely a question of whether help should be provided through the use of legal procedures. Many services to families with children suffering or likely to suffer significant harm are now provided on a so called *voluntary* basis under S17, with both social workers and parents being aware that a failure to co-operate would lead to care proceedings. The impact of a section 47 intervention, though it may be distressing to parents may also be enough to persuade some parents to engage in a process of change. Thoburn, Brandon and Lewis (*1997*) in their research on need, risk and significant harm commented that "there was evidence to suggest that in 33 out of the 76 cases where the child's name was entered on the child protection register, protection and support could have been provided just as successfully, if not more so, outside the formal child protection system, though *in most cases the initial protection conference was probably necessary*" (my italics).

The authors make two important points. First, they found that protecting children did not necessarily also enhance their welfare. Services needed to focus on both objectives. Second, they concluded that the willingness of parents to become involved in the protection process and the degree of danger to the child were major factors to be considered in deciding whether to use the child protection process. This would accord with the views and research findings of Jones (*Chapter 4*) and with the criteria for immediate protection discussed earlier, namely the degree of impairment of the parent's capacity to care, the lack of an acceptable explanation for existing harm and the failure of parents to take any responsibility for what has happened.

There are different stages in the process of assessment and change at which decisions need to be made about the child's future and about the legal framework necessary to achieve this. Figure 2 overleaf describes this process. It is very important to consider time scales for parental change that also reflect the child's needs for change.

Child's Needs	Parental Capacity	Local Authority Action
Has suffered, is suffering or is likely to suffer significant harm	Some strengths, some problems, takes some responsibility for harm, contemplating change	Enquiries and decision, with or without S47 conference, to offer services
Very severe abuse has happened and/or danger of likely serious harm. Child needs protection	Deeply entrenched dysfunctional behaviour/ambivalent or refusing to contemplate change/ takes no responsibility for harm	Accommodation or Emergency Protection Order, or abusing parent leaves home. Offer of services
Continuing need for protection *or* child at home continuing to suffer significant harm and impairment of health & development	Seems unable to change	Commence care proceedings. Continue discussions about possibility of change and provision of services
Child's needs including need for protection can now be met at home **or** Continued risk of significant harm and/or need for protection	Moves through change cycle Little or no change	Care/supervision or possibly no order. Continue services Care order Review service continuation
Plans needed for permanent alternative care either through adoption or long term care	Relapse or no change or insufficient change to meet child's needs.	Care order to enable sharing of parental responsibility and planning

Figure 2

For how long should services be offered?

Crittenden (*1993*) suggests that "assessment of the severity of harm may be seen as the potential of a dynamic system to respond to children's needs". The response will depend on the state of the child, on the parents' capacity to change, and on the resources that can be made available. She suggests that families can be assigned to the following levels of functioning and time scales during which interventions and support would need to be provided:

- *Independent and adequate;*

- *Vulnerable to crisis* – families who need temporary (less than one year) services. The family would then be expected to be able to resume responsibility for managing itself;

- *Restorable* – these are needy families who will require interventions on many levels over a long period of time (two to five years) in order to restore the family to independence;

- *Supportable* – the family needs are so great in relation to family competence and available intervention technologies that there will need to be long-term intervention over many years to enable parents to rear their children successfully;

- *Inadequate* – essential family needs in this situation cannot be met by current services and the children must be placed in alternative homes.

It is clear from these criteria that short periods of intervention may not be enough for some families. Decision about the length of time a service may be provided should be closely related to what is happening to the child. Continuing abuse or severe impairment of health and development should not be tolerated. Parental care should be good enough, with the assistance of supports and services, to meet the child's needs within a space of three to six months but the families in the restorable and supportable groups will, as Crittenden states, then need continuing services for much longer periods in order to make changes in other aspects of their functioning and to be able to sustain these changes.

It will be very much harder to place children and help them to develop adequately if decisions are delayed . The effects of earlier harm are likely to be compounded rather than resolved. Help needs to be offered to vulnerable children and families when the children are still very young or immediately after the referral and assessment of older children who were not previously known to professionals. Diagnoses of actual or likely significant harm needs to be made early on in the contact between professionals and families. Early diagnosis and the provision of support need to be followed by rapid decision-making, if situations do not change, in order to stop harm becoming chronic and therefore more likely to have unfavourable outcomes for the child. Children cannot wait for long periods in harmful or in limbo situations in the hope that their parents may ultimately change.

The realisation at the outset that a family may require services for a period of years will create dilemmas for managers of budgets similar to those already experienced in the National Health Service. Rationing resources for all families is unlikely to facilitate better care for children. Social service departments need to develop criteria for determining which families can have the resources they need. Other agencies, courts, communities, and families should be aware of the criteria.

The known effectiveness of services is likely to be an important con-sideration. For example, studies on the effectiveness of preventive services suggest that it is important to make an early diagnosis of the severity of parental difficulties. Daro, (1996) reviewing the last decade of work in the USA, commented that it had been very hard for workers to accept that there was a core group of families who could not respond to the preventive services on offer. These families did not improve; they caused staff burn out and they prevented other families from benefiting from services. These parents are likely to be similar to the ones identified by Jones (*Chapter 4*).

Conclusion

It is clear that there has often been great difficulty in achieving the balance between protection and services to children in need envisaged in the Children Act 1989. The emphasis has been on child protection and investigations of incidents of abuse; childrens' other needs have not been attended to. As part of the search for solutions it has been suggested (*Gibbons, 1997*) that there should be a raising of the threshold for statutory intervention. This would enable a diversion of resources to support services. This seems simplistic and unlikely on its own to achieve the desired aim of meeting the needs of children who have suffered, are suffering or are likely to suffer significant harm. Child protection does not just involve section 47 investigations. Through section 31 it can provide more extended protection for children, a framework for facilitating change and an underpinning for planning the future of children who cannot return home. Moreover there is insufficient understanding at present of what family support means, how it should be used and what is effective in achieving change for both children and families.

To maximise the chance of meeting childrens' welfare needs and promoting change in families there needs to be a professional consensus about the definition of significant harm, an understanding of the process of assessment and of change, a decision-making structure based on an evaluation of the effectiveness of the services provided to achieve the required changes and provision of good quality alternative care for children and young people who cannot return home.

In order to provide these services, staff, as Davies (*1996*) stated, will need knowledge and skills. They will also need training, support and time to do the work. This poses a terrible dilemma for local authorities trying to work within financial constraints. However, unless local authorities recognise first, the need to develop these services in conjunction with the voluntary agencies and the health and education services and secondly, the professional knowledge base, level of skill and human resources required to sustain them, it may not be possible to fulfil the aims of the Children Act in a way that brings real benefit to many children and families.

Bibliography

Cicchetti, D., Toth, S. (1995). A Developmental Psychopathology Perspective on Child Abuse and Neglect. *Journal of Academic Child and Adolescent Psychiatry*, **34**: 5.

Crittenden, P., Claussen, H. (1993). Severity of Maltreatment; assessment and policy implications. In Hobbs C., Wynne J. (Eds.) *Bailliere's Clinical Paediatrics; Child abuse*. Vol 1/Number 1, Bailliere Tyndall.

Daro, D. (1997). Unpublished Paper. APSAC Conference. San Diego.

Davies, C. (1996). Refocusing Children's Services; Objectives and Outcomes. In Armstrong H. (Ed.) *Refocusing Children's Services Conference Department of Health. Association of Directors of Social Services*. DoH – Refocusing Series – 1997.

Department of Health (1998). *Protecting Children. A Guide for Social Workers undertaking a Comprehensive Assessment.*

Department of Health (1994). *The Challenge of Partnership.*

Department of Health (1995). *Child Protection. Messages from Research*. HMSO.

Farmer, E., Owen, M. (1995). *Child Protection Practice: Private Risks and Public Remedies*. HMSO.

Graham, P., Dingwall, R., Wolkind, S. (1985). Research issues in Child Abuse. *Social Science and Medicine*. **21(11)**: 1216–1228.

Gibbons, J. (1997). Relating outcomes to objectives in child protection policy. In Parton, N. (Ed.) *Child Protection and Family Support*. Routledge.

Gough, D. (1993). The case for and against prevention. In Waterhouse, L. (Ed.) *Child Abuse and Child Abusers*. JKP.

James, B. (1989). *Treating Traumatised Children*. Lexington Books.

Jones, D. (1991). The Effectiveness of Intervention. In Adcock, M., White, R., Hollows, A. (Eds.) *Significant Harm*. Significant Publications.

Howe, D. (1992). Theories of helping, empowerment and participation. In Thoburn, J. (Ed.) *Participation in Practice – Involving families in child protection*. University of East Anglia, Norwich.

Kagan, R., Schlosberg, S. (1989). *Families in Perpetual Crisis*. Norton.

Miller, W.R., Rollnick, S. (1991). *Motivational Interviewing*. Guildford Press.

Parker, R.A. (1986). Child Care: The Roots of a Dilemma. *Political Quarterly*. **57(3)**: 305–324.

Morrison, T. Change, control and the legal framework. In Adcock, M., White, R., Hollows, A. (Eds.) (1991). *Significant Harm*. Significant Publications.

Rooney, R. (1988). Socialisation Strategies for Involuntary Clients. *Journal of Contemporary Social Work*.

Sainsbury, E. (1975). *Social Work with Families*. RKP.

Skuse, D., Bentovim, A. (1994). Physical and Emotional Maltreatment. In Rutter M., Taylor, Hersov, L. (Eds.) *Child and Adolescent Psychiatry; Modern Approaches*. 3rd edition.

Thoburn, J., Brandon, M., Lewis, A. (1997). Need, Risk and Significant Harm. In Parton, N. (Ed.) *Child Protection and Family Support*. Routledge.

Thoburn, J., Lewis, A., Shemmings, D. (1995). *Paternalism or Partnership. Family Involvement in the Child Protection Process*. HMSO.

Widom, C. (*in press*). Behavioural Consequences of Child Maltreatment. In Reece, C.M. (Ed.) *The Treatment of Child Abuse*. Baltimore MD. John Hopkins University Press.

CHAPTER THREE:

Significant harm in context

Dr Arnon Bentovim

The notion of significant harm is an essential one in the making of a care or supervision order. It is important to look at what it comprises, and to consider other aspects of the issues involved. Harm itself is now defined not only in terms of traditional notions of ill treatment – that is physical abuse – but also includes sexual abuse which may show no physical effects, and non physical ill treatment such as emotional abuse. It also includes the impairment of health or development where health implies physical or mental health, and development is not only physical, but also includes intellectual, emotional, social or behavioural development.

It may be useful to think of significant harm generally as a compilation of significant events, both acute and long-standing, which interact with the child's ongoing development, and interrupt, alter, or impair physical and psychological development. Being the victim of significant harm is likely to have a profound effect on a child's view of themselves as a person, and on their future lives. Significant harm represents a major symptom of failure of adaptation by parents to their role, and also involves both the family and society.

Categories of harm

It may be useful to think in terms of:

Physical abuse – Physical injury to a child where there is a definite knowledge, or a reasonable suspicion, that the injury was inflicted or not knowingly prevented. This also includes the induction of illness states through the administration of medications, or noxious substances.

Neglect – The persistent or severe neglect of a child which results in serious impairment of that child's health or development. This may take the form of exposure to danger, or repeated failure to attend to the physical and, or developmental needs of a child. An alternative form is failure to thrive without organic cause, resulting from the neglect of a child.

Emotional abuse – The persistent emotional ill treatment of a child which has a severe adverse effect on the behaviour and emotional development of that child.

Sexual abuse – The involvement of dependent, immature children and adolescents in sexual activities that they do not really comprehend, to which they are unable to give informed consent, which violate the social taboos of family life, and are knowingly not prevented by the carer.

Definitions for the purpose of registration can be found in *Working Together* (*1991*) but it is noted in *Working Together* that the definitions offered there "do not tie in precisely with the definition of 'significant harm' in Section 31 of the Children Act".

Levels of abuse

It is helpful to think of each category in terms of the severity of the abuse (*see Figure 1 opposite*).

There is clearly a difference in approaching the least severe forms of abuse. There would be an expectation of agencies working together in such cases with the use of child protection registration, working on a voluntary basis in partnership with parents and a variety of different agencies to offer appropriate assistance. However, even lesser forms of abuse, such as exhibitionism or sexual fondling, can have major implications because the abuse may be associated with a basic paedophiliac orientation, and may require protective action of a different magnitude to a child who has a mild degree of neglect, or is living in a critical scapegoating atmosphere.

Where moderate levels of abuse are present, the implication for the longer term mental and physical health of the child without appropriate intervention is far more doubtful. There may well need to be a higher level of protective action, such as the use of interim care orders or interim supervision orders during a period of longer-term assessment or prohibited steps or specific issues orders may be necessary, in addition to a supervision order.

Least severe	Moderate abuse	Severe abuse
Bruising, no fractures in an older child	Bruising in a baby, fractures not including head and neck	Fractures, multiple, over a period of time, different sites, particularly with fractures around the head and neck in a baby under 6 months
Weight parallel rather than markedly below third centile	Growth failure, but not length, basically of weight	Severe non-organic failure to thrive with stunting in both length and weight
Mild degrees of neglect without major failure to care, and family chaos	Failure of care, moderate degrees of deprivation and neglect	Severe neglect, deprivation state, skin, hair changes, severe accidents due to poor supervision
Critical, scapegoating, confusing atmosphere, emotional disorder without major conduct problems	Rejection, privation but with tendencies towards conduct problems rather than frozen regression and retardation	Severe rejection resulting in pseudo-autistic, regresses states of frozen watchfulness, pseudo-retardation
Sexual exhibitionism	Sexual abuse, shorter duration, fondling and/or oral contact	Sexual abuse, long-standing, involving attempted or actual genital or anal intercourse, particularly in younger children associated with gross physical signs, major sexualised patterns
	Fabrication of symptoms leading to investigation	Induction of illness of such severity that life is threatened – e.g. suffocation, attempted drowning

Figure 1

Severe abuse is also going to require higher levels of protection during the assessment process. There are likely to be cases where care orders or residence orders and carefully managed contact will be necessary.

Psychosocial difficulties associated with significant harm

Patterns of abusive behaviour or harmful attitudes may develop in parents as a result of the interaction of the intellectual and emotional characteristics and behaviour of the parent(s) and the demand of the child and the outside world at a particular time. In understanding a particular case, family attributes and parental care must be assessed in terms of the possibility of change: and the potential for providing adequate competent care in the future. It is usual to consider the physical and psychiatric health of the parents, and to define any adult psychiatric syndromes present. The intellectual potential of the parents, their functioning and parenting ability must also be considered. Assessment must be made of their ability to provide an adequate affective atmosphere, warmth, nurturance and a caring relationship. The patterns of alliances that are created within the family, and the expectations of family members, must be considered along with the boundaries of the family, that is, the parents' capacity to maintain the line between themselves and the child, and their ability to communicate and share with the children. Further aspects of the assessment should include parents' competence in carrying out tasks, their ability to relate to professionals in the outside world, and their relationship with neighbourhood and extended family.

Mrazek et al (*1995*) in attempting to assess parenting risks considered the following issues to be important:-

- How emotionally available is the parent, that is what is the degree of emotional warmth displayed?

- How appropriate are the controls used by the parent, how flexible and permissive versus restrictive and punitive is the parent?

- How psychiatrically disturbed is the parent? Is there any particular form of disorder present, what type of disorder, and how severe are the overt symptoms?

- What is the knowledge basis that the parent has? How well does the parent understand emotional, physical development and child care principles?

- How committed is the parent to the child? Are child care responsibilities adequately prioritised in the general life of the family?

They also consider parenting on a risk scale of 'adequate', 'concerns about parenting' and 'parenting difficulties'.

Recognised stress factors which may contribute to physical harm or psychiatric disturbance in the child and therefore to significant emotional harm include:

- parental psychiatric disturbance;

- discordant intrafamilial relations;

- lack of warmth in intrafamilial relations;

- familial over involvement;

- inadequate or inconsistent parental control;

- inadequate living conditions;

- inadequate or distorted intrafamilial communications;

- anomalous family situations.

All of these and a variety of other major stressful factors can affect parental behaviour, and result in over-punitive attitudes, rejection, escalation of aversive, negative interactions, and perception of the child as deserving rejection or abuse.

Family health scales have been developed to describe family functions (*Kinston et al, 1987*). There are a number of areas which specifically focus on parenting. Figure 2 illustrates these. There are four levels of functioning. Optimal and adequate functioning describe family contexts which should be good enough to ensure appropriate nurturance and adequate socialisation. Dysfunctional and breakdown levels describe contexts which put children at serious risk of significant harm if they continue and the standard of care does not improve.

	Breakdown	**Dysfunctional**
Pattern of relationships	Serious deficiencies; marked splits, scapegoating, severe triangulation, or isolation of all family members	Serious discord or distance between members, or shifting or exclusive alignments. Children repeatedly detour parental tension or conflicts.
Marital relationship	Destructive relationship, for example, couple fused, at war or isolated from one another	Overt marital difficulties; or both partners dissatisfied
Parental relationship	Parents not working together at all, or extremely weak, divisive or conflicted relationship	Parents repeatedly disagree, act without reference to one another, or one parent repeatedly takes over or opts out
Parent–child relationship	Both parents reject, ignore, exploit, continuously attack or disqualify a child	Parental attitudes and behaviours are clearly unsupportive or harmful; poor understanding of the children
Child–parent relationship	Children avoid, reject, continually oppose, or cling to parent(s); or show marked differentiation in their attitudes to each parent	One of more children show oppositional, withdrawn, over-dependent or domineering behaviour towards parent(s)
Sibling relationships	Sibs fight continuously or ignore each other; extreme rivalry and competition for the parents' attention	Obvious discord or distance between the sibs

Adequate	Optimal
Satisfactory relationships but with greater closeness or distance between some family members than others	The nature and strength of relationships between family members is constructive and appropriate to their respective ages and roles
Basically satisfactory with some areas of discontent	Mature relationship; warm, supportive, affectionate, emphatic, compatible; couple work together well
Basic agreement on child-rearing but with some deficiencies in support and/or working together	Strong parental coalition; agreement and cooperation in child-rearing; sharing of pleasure and mutual support
Parents support children and enjoy being with them but with minor or occasional problems in relating to the children	Parents show care and concern; understand and pay attention to children appropriately; and are ready to participate in their activities
Child–parent relationships are secure, but with mild difficulties in some areas or between particular dyads	Children relate to both parents; are cooperative yet spontaneous; feel safe and show appropriate dependence
Sibs affiliate with some limited rivalry, quarrelling or lack of contact	Sibs interact freely with shared enjoyment, affection, concern; differences can be resolved

Figure 2

Descriptions from the 'Alliances mainscale' of the family health scales, which considers the relationships and coalitions amongst family members (Kinston et al 1987).

Understanding and establishing significant harm

To understand and establish the significant harm criteria in Section 31 it is necessary to consider:

1. The family context in which significant harm occurs.

2. The process of the development of the child in this context.

3. The nature of significant harm in terms of ill treatment and its effects on development with or without intervention.

4. The nature of significant impairment which includes developmental issues, physical factors, parental contributions, and other factors and comparison with a similar child.

5. The link with an assessment of parental care, and what it is reasonable to expect of parents.

The family context and significant harm

The family is an organisation which has grown up to meet the needs of the individuals within it. Competent partnering implies the meeting of adult needs for support, affection and sexuality and competent parenting implies the provision of adequate nurturance, care, warmth, stimulation and socialisation of children.

A 'Good Enough' parent provides:

• adequate verbal communication to give information and intellectual stimulation;

• sufficient physical freedom to encourage the development of the child's sensory and motor abilities;

• adequate responsiveness which balances the child's need for attention to his or her behaviour, and the needs of the parent;

• positive warmth and a loving framework.

This tempers the child's demands and helps the child learn to be self regulatory rather than requiring external monitoring (*Maccoby and Martin, 1983*).

It is important to consider the nature of the family and to see it as an organisation which has strengths to nurture, care and socialise, but also to be aware of inherent problems within the organisation which make it liable to develop interactions which can be sufficiently harmful to require professional intervention.

Families are prone to stress. Families are constantly undergoing changes or transitions. The life cycle, birth of children, maturation, ageing, retirement and death, represent major events which can have effects on the family and on the parents' capacity to care. Similarly, events affecting individuals, e.g. unemployment, illness, handicap, may cause stress to be transmitted to other family members. Violent means of dealing with stress is a characteristic learned response and may be transmitted within the family. The question is not whether the family is an institution prone to violence and conflict, but how much there is and whether the effects create a family context which is significantly harmful to the children within it. Gelles and Strauss (*1979*) have pinpointed a number of such factors in their research.

Privacy

The modern family is a private institution, isolated from the eyes, the ears and often enough the rules of wider society. Social control by definition must, therefore, be low. Idiosyncratic rules and family meanings grow in isolation. Appropriate ways of expressing both violence and affection within the community can be distorted by personal interpretation and enacted in the family with little external influence. Although there is public outcry about mistreatment of children, there is still a reluctance to interfere in family life.

Development of the child

The unfolding of the various aspects of development is complex. Constitutional, genetic and environmental factors, e.g. the effects of physical illness, injury and handicapping conditions and the family context in which the child grows up all play a part. Culture, class factors and intergenerational effects which derive from the parents' own experiences of parenting may also be influential.

Current views on development (*see Cicchetti and Toth, 1995*) emphasise that what matters for development is that the various systems – biological and psychological – should be well integrated. Development is about progression, change and reorganisation throughout life. Significant harm occurs because of a disruption of the tasks to be achieved at particular ages and stages of development. In normal development we see consolidation and growth at each stage; in significant harm new forms of maladaption and vulnerability. The key areas to be concerned about in considering development and significant harm are as follows:

- The regulations of feelings

- The development of attachments

- The development of a sense of self

- Making adequate peer relationships

- Adaptation to school

- Long term mental and physical health

The regulation of feelings

This is to do with the way in which a child's arousal and distress becomes directed, controlled, modulated and modified to enable the child to function in all sorts of contexts including those which are potentially stressful. An adequately parented infant will demonstrate a resilient control of intense feelings in a variety of contexts. By contrast physically abused infants demonstrate high levels of negative feelings, and little positive, whilst an emotionally neglected infant presents as blunted, with little negative or positive feelings. Such feelings states persist and are noted during pre-school and junior school where such children are rated as being over-active and distractible, inattentive and aggressive. Such children relate to their peers with anger, fear and aggression, rather than concern for others and emotional responsiveness. The failure to manage feelings because of the overwhelmingly negative nature of emotions associated with significant harm also has a highly negative effect on forming attachments.

The development of attachments

Children form models and a map of themselves and significant others based on their relationship history. Their feelings, their understandings and expectations about the future are organised and carried forward into future relationships on the basis of the ones that have been made early in their lives. There is a strong association between significant harm and insecure attachments (*Ainsworth, 1980; Egelund and Sroufe, 1991; Crittenden, 1988*). Carlson et al (*1989*) found that more than 80% of significantly harmed infants had disorganised attachments compared to less than 20% in a normal comparison group. Barnett et al (*1992*) found that 60% of those infants classified as disorganised in their pattern of attachment relationship at the age of 12 months, had the same classification a year later.

Although these patterns gradually modify as children mature and meet other significant adults in their lives, a considerable number of significantly harmed children between 7–13 describe themselves as not feeling close to anyone, and feeling confused about their relationships. Thus, maltreated children are at considerable risk. This pattern arises because of the inconsistent care which is the common element in all significant harm. Negative expectations arise, expecting the worst of new relationships. As a result such children can be controlling to avoid disaster. The importance for the future is that when such children become parents, if they have managed to work through and resolve early aversive experiences, they are not likely to engage in a repetition of a pattern of maltreatment to their own children. But if as adults they are still preoccupied and living in the past, or assert that their past is without significance, then there is a risk that maladaptive parenting practices will develop.

The development of the self

As children become more aware of themselves during the second year, they are able to use their capacities to play and communicate to convey their needs and feelings. But the relationship offered in response has a significant impact on how the child's sense of themselves develops. Even as toddlers, there are indications that significantly harmed children will have a negative response towards themselves in comparison to children who have not experienced significant harm. Children who have been well cared for can talk accurately about their feelings of hunger, thirst, anger, or hate and bad feelings. But children subject to significant harm do not seem to be able to define how they feel about themselves or others, and being made the subject of negative responses, seems to inhibit such expressions. In later childhood there is a general effect of significantly harmed children having highly negative views of themselves, lower self esteem, perceiving themselves not to be competent, and to be prone to depression and pervasive sadness.

Peer relationships

The two main effects of significant harm in general on peer relationships are those of showing physical and verbal aggression, including responding with anger and aggression to friendly overtures and signs of distress in others. The other observation has been a high degree of withdrawal and avoidance of peer relationships. This seems to be an active strategy of avoidance, leading to increasing isolation (*Mueller and Silverman, 1989*).

The experience of being maltreated thus leads children along different pathways to peer rejection and isolation. The confluence of negative representational models of attachment figures, and of the self, and the self in relationship to others, makes maltreated children extremely vulnerable to functioning maladaptively in peer relationships and school related issues (*Cicchetti and Toth, 1995*).

Adaptation to school

The school environment exerts direct effects on educational achievement, and skills that are acquired in the elementary grades serve as a foundation for success in higher education, and future employment opportunities (*Silva, 1994*). Understanding of social relationships and emotional responsiveness also emerge out of the school environment, so that adaptation to school, including integration into the peer group, acceptable classroom performance and orientation for achievement, is a process which is important for all children. The child's experience in the home provides an important foundation on which the transition to the school setting is built. Children who have been maltreated are at high risk for failure in school, so that a potentially positive experience that could serve to reverse an early trajectory of maladaptation more often confirms the maltreated child's negative history and maladaptive relationship patterns.

Physically abused children prove to be aggressive, non compliant, acting out, and function more poorly on cognitive tasks (*Erickson et al, 1989*). Neglected children have severe and variable school difficulties, and are often described as anxious, inattentive, unable to understand their work, lacking in initiative, and heavily dependent on teachers. They rarely express positive feelings or show a sense of humour. Sexually abused children are unpopular, anxious, inattentive, and unable to understand expectations. Such children have lower grades, they do not establish secure relationships, and are over concerned with issues of security, due to an expectation of unresponsivity and rejection from adults. All aspects of the school environment provide difficulties for maltreated children and failure occurs very readily (*Eckenrode et al, 1993*), although there are some children who appear to sink themselves into learning as an attempt to avoid having to think about home stresses.

Long term mental and physical health

Disruptions in achieving developmental steps in earlier areas also has an implication for the child's functioning across his or her life span. Developmental liabilities may become enduring vulnerability factors that increase the risk for emergence of physical and mental health problems. Maltreated children have elevated levels of disturbance across a wide range of areas, rather than in any specific field (*Aber et al, 1989*). Physical abuse is associated with child depressive symptomatology, conduct disorder and delinquency, and there are higher rates of diagnoses of Attention Deficit Hyperactivity Disorder, Oppositional Disorder, and Post Traumatic Stress Disorder, noted generally amongst maltreated children. There are links noted with anti-social personality disorders, substance abuse, suicidal and self injurious behaviour, somatising, anxiety, depression and dissociation and attachment disorders (*Luntz and Widon, 1994*). Thus across childhood and into adulthood, maltreatment and significant harm poses an increased risk for a wide range of disturbances in functioning. This in turn affects parental roles and adult functioning.

Parenting roles and identification

Associated with major disruption of attachments is the induction of children into particular roles within the family, and the need for the child to respond to particular relationship demands. Individuals who themselves have had major deficits in their own parenting characteristically see in the birth of a new baby a hope both of a child to love, and to make up for past failures. There may be an expectation that the child will supply the emotional needs not met through earlier life experiences or through relationship with a partner. Alternatively women with an absence of good memories of their own childhood may focus their lives on caretaking and put the care of others and the care of their own children ahead of their need as partners in their adult relationship (*Monck et al, 1996*).

The danger is that children, because of their own needs can make demands that overwhelm the resources of such parents. This means that frustration, resentment and grievance are almost inevitable. There is a risk of rejection, abuse and a recreation of the very pattern of abuse the parent had been avoiding (*Crittenden & Bonvillian, 1984*).

The significance of harm

Significant harm may be defined as the state of a child which is attributable to ill treatment or failure to provide adequate care. To understand and demonstrate the significance of the harm, we have to consider in detail the effect of ill treatment and inadequate care on the child's development. There is no specific pattern of response to particular forms of maltreatment, but there are non specific signs and symptoms of developmental deviation resulting from the child's trauma.

Significant harm can be seen as the effects of ill treatment and poor care on the potential of the child to develop along the lines described earlier in comparison with the development of a similar child. Significant harm may also represent a traumatic event in the child's life.

Trauma is a Greek word meaning 'to pierce'. It is most often used in the context of physical injury, where the skin is broken – where something once intact has been breached. It suggests that the event which creates the breach is of a certain intensity or violence – and consequences to the organism are long standing. From the physical notion of trauma arises the notion of trauma as an event which in the same intense or violent way ruptures the protective layer that surrounds the mind, with equally long lasting consequences for psychic organisation (*Garland, 1991*).

A sense of helplessness overwhelms the individual; mastery, control and defence fails, and there is a sense of being unprotected, of disintegration and acute mental pain. Although significant harm can take the form of acute single overwhelming events, they are often repeated, frequent and in a context of rejection, anger and failure to respond to the core of the child's being.

Traumatic events are a specific form of severe stress – where stress is defined as a "disequilibratory event which temporarily disturbs the functioning of the individual and initiates a chain of adaptive or maladaptive responses" (*Wolfe, 1987*). Pynoos and Eth (*1985*) have described the Post Traumatic Stress Disorder in children, which is defined as responses to particular events.

1. The traumatic event is persistently re-experienced in at least one of recurrent intrusive and distressing recollections or dreams, re-experiencing action or feelings (traumatic play), extensive distress at reminders.

2. There may be a persistent avoidance of stimuli associated with trauma or numbing of general responsiveness.

3. There may be persistent symptoms of increased arousal, irritability, sleep difficulties, excessive vigilance, started response, reactions to reminders of stress.

4. Usually the onset is immediately following the traumatic event.

Trauma can be longstanding and associated with extreme stress. It is associated with very strong denial and dissociation; extensive numbing; self doubt, insecurity, elevated fears, anxiety and a sense of rage which bursts through at times; and an unremitting sense of sadness as personality style (*Terr, 1971*).

The infant and growing child has to adapt and cope with these experiences to survive psychologically. Personal constructions or attributions have to be formed in a search for meanings for uncontrollable events. Children may either blame themselves or some feature or person in the outside world. Abnormal attachment patterns, ambivalent clinging and fighting, aversive turning away from the parent, the dazed, anxious or disorientated attitude of the disruptive child, all represent ways of coping. Such distorted patterns of relating come to be represented in the child's mind as a 'model of the world' and to organise his way of responding (*Crittenden, 1988*).

Psychologically children may have to develop a shell implying total self sufficiency, so that throughout the stages of development when the child should be becoming peer worthy and relating to other adults, he presents himself as being without needs and may be seen as aloof, distant and without empathy. This has devastating effects on the long term ability to relate both as a child, young person and later as a parent (*Bentovim & Kinston, 1991*).

Another response may be the compliant, victim role associated with a process of identification with the aggressor. The child may appear to seek punishment, and as time goes on, become involved in relationships which perpetuate abuse.

A distressing response may be that of identification with the abuser. The child becomes manipulative, controlling, hostile, and combative instead of responsive and receptive.

Figure 3 shows the way in which such traumatic experiences can affect the childhood and adolescence of individuals and their ability to be parents to their own children in subsequent generations. To be competent, parenting requires the development of empathy; the ability to be able to read the emotional cues of the other; to put ones own needs

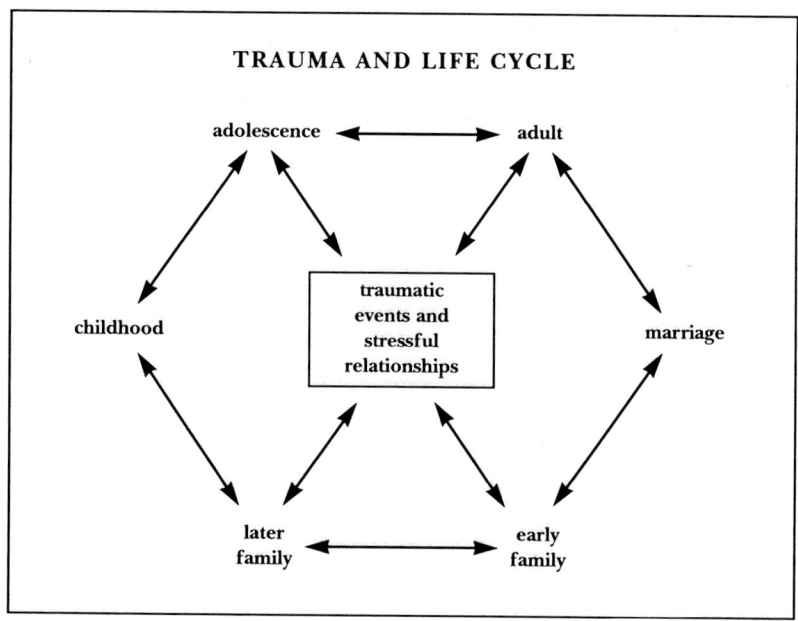

Figure 3

aside and focus on the needs of children; to be appropriately firm and ensure that social rules are learnt and maintained. The long term experience of abuse during childhood and adolescence may affect the development of these parental skills in a devastating way. It can result in an authoritarian style of parenting, insensitivity to the child's level of ability, or needs, combined with the excessive demands, use of power and assertive techniques which are characteristic of physically abusive parents (*La Rose & Wolfe, 1987*).

Protective factors

There are protective factors which can mitigate against such responses and there is a significant degree of plasticity or resilience in development (*Rutter, 1983*). This depends in part on the response of significant adults and their ability to exert control and efficacy in the midst of confusion and upheaval. It depends too on the earlier history, for example, of attachments, which may have provided a rehearsal and practice for later defences against stressful events (*Lipsett, 1983*). Intervention, treatment, placement in positive environments, even the making of more satisfactory relationships in adulthood can neutralise some of the potentially harmful long term effects. Not all physically, or sexually, abused children become abusive adults although there is a higher risk (3–5 times as high) in comparison with adults who were not abused.

Significant harm and physical abuse

Significant physical harm occurs either as a result of neglect or failure to care, implying a failure of protection on the parents' part, or the commission of physical harm through inappropriate punitiveness, or desire to hurt and inflict pain. Physical abuse usually occurs in a context of an abusive atmosphere within the home. High levels of punitiveness, unexpected pain and hurt, the misuse of power and authority involved in physical abuse also have major effects on the behavioural pattern of the child (*Maccoby & Martin, 1983*). Figure 4 shows the effects of frequent misuse of power (*Spinetta and Rigler, 1972*).

There is a connection between the sense of powerlessness, resulting from invasion of the body, vulnerability, absence of protection and a repeated fear and helplessness. This can result in fear, anxiety and an inability to control events, along with learning difficulties, despair, depression and low sense of efficacy seen as 'frozen watchfulness'. This sense of helplessness may lead to the development of a need to control and dominate, or to aggressive, abusive patterns, or the development of 'a shell' to ward off feelings about the other person (*George & Main, 1979*).

Behaviours indicative of poor self control have been described by Gaensbauer & Sands (*1979*). They include distractibility, negative emotions, low enthusiasm and resistance to direction.

Within the school, patterns of behaviour may include attention seeking, extremely provocative behaviour to adults and bullying. Ultimately there may be a major rejection of the child. Such behavioural patterns are grouped together as the psychiatric disorder of 'conduct problems'. The children are perceived as difficult to manage, less socially mature, rejected by peers, deficient in social skills, and liable to commit violent criminal acts (*Herrenkohl et al, 1984*).

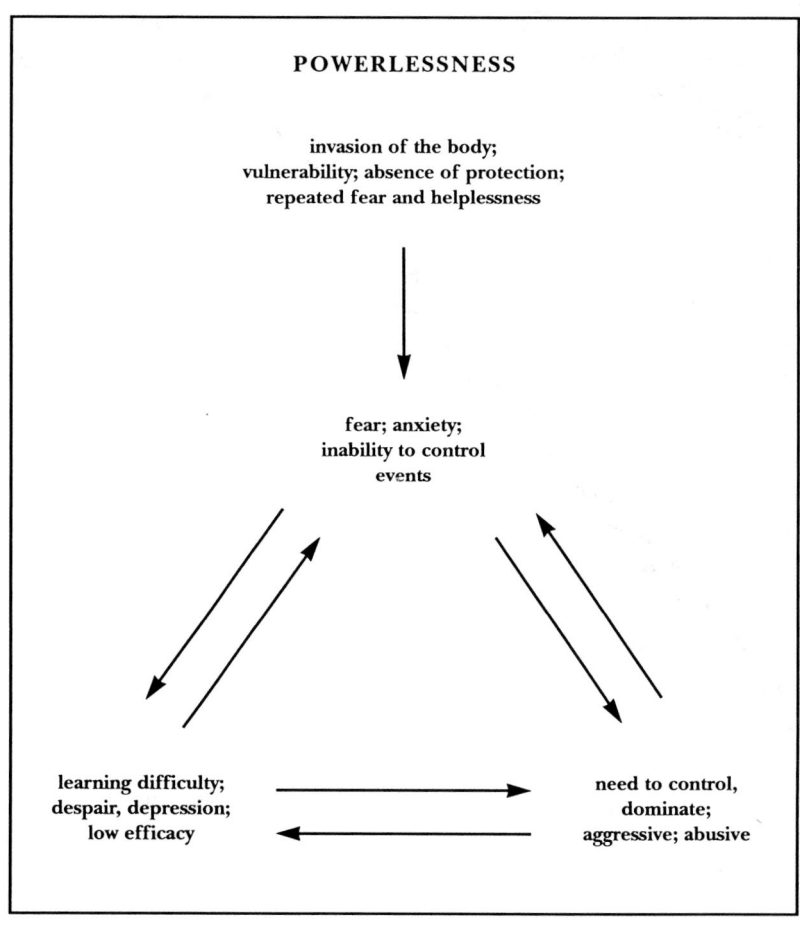

POWERLESSNESS

**invasion of the body;
vulnerability; absence of protection;
repeated fear and helplessness**

**fear; anxiety;
inability to control
events**

**learning difficulty;
despair, depression;
low efficacy**

**need to control,
dominate;
aggressive; abusive**

Figure 4

If moderate or severe abuse continues over a long period, responses may be seen such as depressive states, hopelessness, self injurious behaviour, pica, enuresis and encopresis.

When describing physical abuse it is essential to bear in mind the effect of the 'abusive context'. The atmosphere of punitiveness, rejection, criticism, scapegoating, belittling, may in turn induce the frozen compliant response, or the provocative angry response which justifies the parents' continuing criticism and anger. There may be perpetuation of the cycle through bullying of other children. Furthermore, there is evidence from epidemiological surveys to show the effect of punitiveness in one generation being repeated in terms of a propensity to use bullying or physically punitive responses in the next generation. These children may be seen as 'out of control' or rejecting parental care (*Gelles & Strauss, 1979*).

Significant harm and emotional abuse

Emotional abuse is sometimes also associated with emotional neglect and may take many forms. It can take the form of a lack of care of physical needs, a failure to provide consistent love and nurture, and also overt hostility and rejection. The long term consequences on social, emotional, cognitive and behavioural development may be far reaching and profound if the child is habitually subject to verbal harassment, or if the child is disparaged, criticised, threatened and ridiculed. The inversion of love by substituting rejection and withdrawal for affection, verbal and non verbal is the epitome of emotional abuse and neglect.

Garbarino et al (*1978*) define emotional or psychological abuse as the destruction of the child's competence to be able to function in social situations. Being denied appropriate contact with peers within or outside school, and being forced to take on a particular role in relation to parents, can therefore be seen as having a major destructive effect on the child's competence to function in social contexts. Glaser (*1995*) describes qualitative dimensions, to include persistent, negative inaccurate attributions; emotional unavailability, unresponsiveness or neglect; failure to recognise individuality and boundary; inconsistent expectation and mis-socialisations.

Parents can feel as if they are the abused children rather than vice versa. Children can be inducted into parental caretaking roles, and may not be encouraged to be involved in appropriate play, relationships with peers, and development of a true self. The extreme of the parental role occurs when there is incestuous abuse and the use of the child as a sexual partner whether by father or mother, inducting the male or female child into a parental or partner role inappropriately (*Bentovim et al, 1988*).

In marital breakdown one parent may use a child as partner against the other parent, and the attachment relationship is disrupted with the other parent. There is a potential for the creation of a rejecting, resentful, relationship with that other parent with blaming and fault finding destroying what may have been a good enough relationship. Accusations of abuse by the other parent can further undermine the potential for developing a secure attachment with both parents, despite separations. It is important to consider whether such situations result in the child suffering significant harm.

When parents have a psychiatric illness a major concern is the adult's involvement of the child in their psychotic process, such as a shared delusionary state or paranoid beliefs (*Rutter, 1966*).

Adaptation to parental lifestyles may also cause significant harm, e.g. where children become part of a parents' drug culture, prostitution or other antisocial activities, and become confused in terms of socialisation into the appropriate moral views of what are appropriate societal values. The boundary between a lifestyle and airing the family beliefs versus being persuaded to use drugs, become prostituted, or involved in direct antisocial acts, may be a fine one, and depends on a comprehensive assessment of the child and family.

Significant harm and physical neglect

Physical Neglect comprises both a lack of both physical care taking and supervision and a failure to fulfil the developmental needs of the child in terms of cognitive stimulation. Severe neglect is associated with major retardation of cognitive functioning and growth, and is recognised through a typical pattern of poor hair growth (skin effects), poor hygiene, withdrawal and in extreme states a pseudo-autistic state, all of which can rapidly reverse in alternative care. These states are associated with the sense of parental hopelessness and helplessness as described by Polansky et al (*1981*). There is often a striking reversal of neglect when the child is in a different context, and the question has to be asked whether a parent can be helped through his or her sense of helplessness towards a new ability to provide adequate stimulation to ensure growth and development rather than failure and deprivation. Professionals, like parents, may feel helpless and overwhelmed by large families living in very poor conditions, with very little social support.

Significant harm and illness induction

Munchausen Syndrome, where adults either medicate themselves or describe symptoms, which can then result in medical investigation or surgical intervention, can also be seen in the child. In recent years there has been major concern about children who are actually induced into illness states by the administration of medications (non accidental poisoning, *Rogers et al, 1976*) or are perceived and described as having symptoms which require investigation, particularly fits and faints: Munchausen Syndrome by Proxy (*Meadow, 1982*).

In recent years a number of reports of deliberate suffocation of children have been published, e.g. Southall et al (*1987*). The commonest form is smothering in which the abuser, usually the child's mother, uses a pillow or similar object to cause mechanical obstruction to the child's airways. The condition presents in infancy, either as an alleged apnoeic attack or, in the most serious cases, an apparent cot death or Sudden Infant Death Syndrome (SIDS). There may be a substantially increased risk to siblings of the victim. Bools and Meadows (*1991*) confirmed earlier work by Rogers et al (*1976*) in seeing the parents as requiring an ill child for their own marital or personal mental health needs.

Gray and Bentovim (*1996*) noted a deeply ambivalent view of the child and an apparently close relationship between mother and child, but on closer examination there is observed to be a deeply anxious form of attachment. The mother and a few fathers appear to construct an illness scenario together with doctors, who are keen to ensure that physical symptoms are fully investigated. There is a desire that the child should be cared for, and the fictitious illness investigated, yet at the same time there is a desire to maintain the illness state and continue putting the child at risk as a way of solving other major individual and family problems. Being in hospital, caring for a sick child, gives 'care by proxy' to the parent.

A child subject to repeated unnecessary medical investigations may suffer unnecessary pain and risk, and if inappropriate treatments are given, they can have dangerous side effects – a manifestation of significant harm. For a child to see themselves as having a major handicapping condition or disability or take on an invalid role where there is a normal potential for health is also a cause of significant harm.

It is essential to understand the processes which lead to this unusual abusive action, so that there can be an assessment of the capacity of the parent to acknowledge the degree of potential harm, and to use appropriate help to be able to nurture and protect the child and to be able to reverse harmful effects.

Significant harm, growth and development

A diagnosis of failure to thrive can only be made if it can be shown that there has been a failure to give sufficient nutrition. Skuse (*1991*) has drawn attention to the fact that considerable care must be exercised in making the diagnosis as there are many other factors which can result in failure to grow as well as failure to provide adequate nutrition. Skuse (*1991*) has also indicated that what is now called retardation of linear growth in older children, formerly known as psychosocial dwarfism, needs to be differentiated from failure to thrive.

Skuse (*1993*) has recently described this condition as Hyperphagic Short Stature, to indicate that these children in fact often eat voraciously, e.g. from dustbins or eating their way through the contents of a refrigerator. Because of the failure of growth hormone due to emotional rejection, the food is not digested in a form which can lead to growth. Major retardation of linear growth can show a reversal in another context. In hospital and foster homes there can often be a quite striking growth, with a considerable acceleration and growth catching up.

Failure to thrive babies respond well to the provision of nutrition by tube feeding or by different handling of feeding. The test is whether the parent can ensure that the child can continue growing and thriving. There is now evidence (*Skuse, 1991*) that prolonged growth failure during the early years has a detrimental affect on brain development. This is shown by failure in the development of cognitive abilities and achieving the potential intellectual level. This represents significant harm to the child. There may well be failure within school and there is a well tested association between conduct problems and learning difficulties within school, e.g. reading, and educational failure.

Sexual abuse

The traumatic effects of child sexual abuse can be summarised by stating that there are multiple affective, cognitive and behavioural effects and such effects persist. The earlier the disruptions occur, the more adversely subsequent phases of development may be affected. The child develops coping mechanisms which were described earlier, for example, shell development to avoid thinking, a compliant victim role, or angry aggressive responses which become stable and result in personality disorders, which shape later relationships and future mental health.

The immediate post-traumatic stress disorder associated with sexual abuse was described by McCleer et al (*1988*) from a series of young children who had been abused within a day nursery. The descriptions are as follows:

- re-experiencing, where children were observed to talk about abuse, playing out abusive patterns;

- flashbacks and nightmares;

- indulging in inappropriate sexual activity;

- memories occurring in places or with people and objects associated with the abuse and considered to be symbolic of them;

- visualisation, drawing, day dreaming their experiences;

- avoidant responses associated with the avoidance of people, places and things associated with abuse.

Children were often fearful of going into particular houses or rooms, or were fearful of people who reminded the child of the abuser, perhaps of a particular gender, e.g. dislike of men or older people. Associated with this was an often extreme unwillingness to talk about abuse, and evidence of deletion – a hole in the mind – and a total lack of memory, even wiping out of memories earlier than the abuse itself.

The children also had difficulties falling or staying asleep, often associated with anxieties about going to sleep, irritable aggressive behaviour which was a reversal of the previous passive sense of having to be involved with abuse, distractibility and difficulty in concentrating and a degree of hyperalertness shown by anxiety or being easily startled. (These symptoms are described as autonomic hyperarousal).

Longer term effects of sexual abuse

The longer abuse continues, the more extensive it is, for example involving penetrative abuse, the older the child, and the greater the number of stages that abuse continues through, the more disturbed the child is likely to be, the more depressed and sad, and the greater their loss of self esteem. Self esteem is the way in which an individual thinks of himself, for example how good or how bad he is. Children who have suffered chronic long-term sexual abuse feel very negatively about themselves and all aspects of their relationships, and they have very high levels of distress (*Monck et al, 1996; Friedrich, 1990; Terr, 1991*).

Longer term effects can be described in terms of what Finkelhor (*1987*) has called traumagenic dynamics (*Figure 5*). Traumatic sexualisation enlarges the traumatic effects described earlier and leads to a cycle of avoidance of anything to do with sexuality, bursts of flashbacks and re-experiencing which continue for many years, sexual pre-occupations, and sexually inappropriate behaviour with other children and adults.

As indicated in Figure 6 girls and boys tend to respond differently to the effects of abuse (*Bentovim, 1992*). Girls follow a female 'mode' internalising their response to abuse. They blame themselves, they attribute sexual abusive action to some aspect of themselves, often reinforced by the abuser who perceives the child's affection to be a sexual invitation. Thus a victim mode with compliant responses is more likely. There is a tendency to hurt and damage themselves with self mutilation, self harm and anxiety and depression. The use of the term 'mode' is used to illustrate the point that although this is a female pathway, some boys may follow the same process, and vice versa.

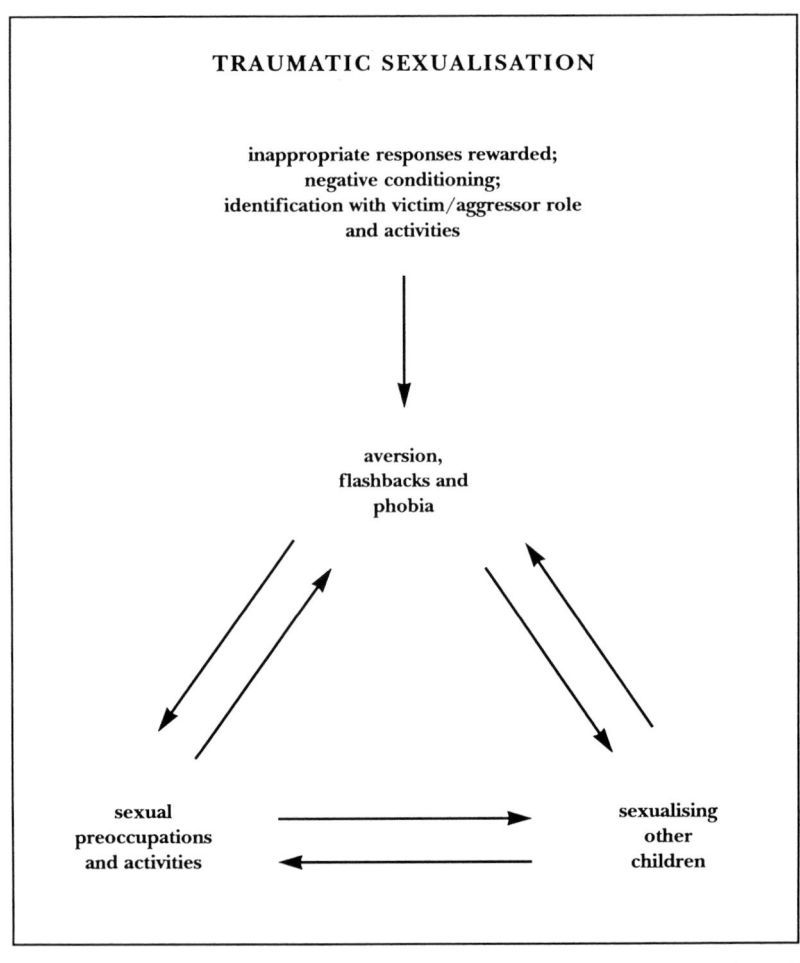

TRAUMATIC SEXUALISATION

inappropriate responses rewarded;
negative conditioning;
identification with victim/aggressor role
and activities

aversion,
flashbacks and
phobia

sexual
preoccupations
and activities

sexualising
other
children

Figure 5

Boys generally follow a male mode and externalise their responses, look for somebody else to blame and take over their negative self representation. They find someone younger to abuse who reminds them of their own powerlessness and develop an abusive, hostile, aggressive style of relating, with conduct disorders and substance abuse. Some girls may also follow this 'male' mode response.

Boys are more likely to adopt a sexually abusive orientation if they have been physically abused as well as sexually abused in their own families,

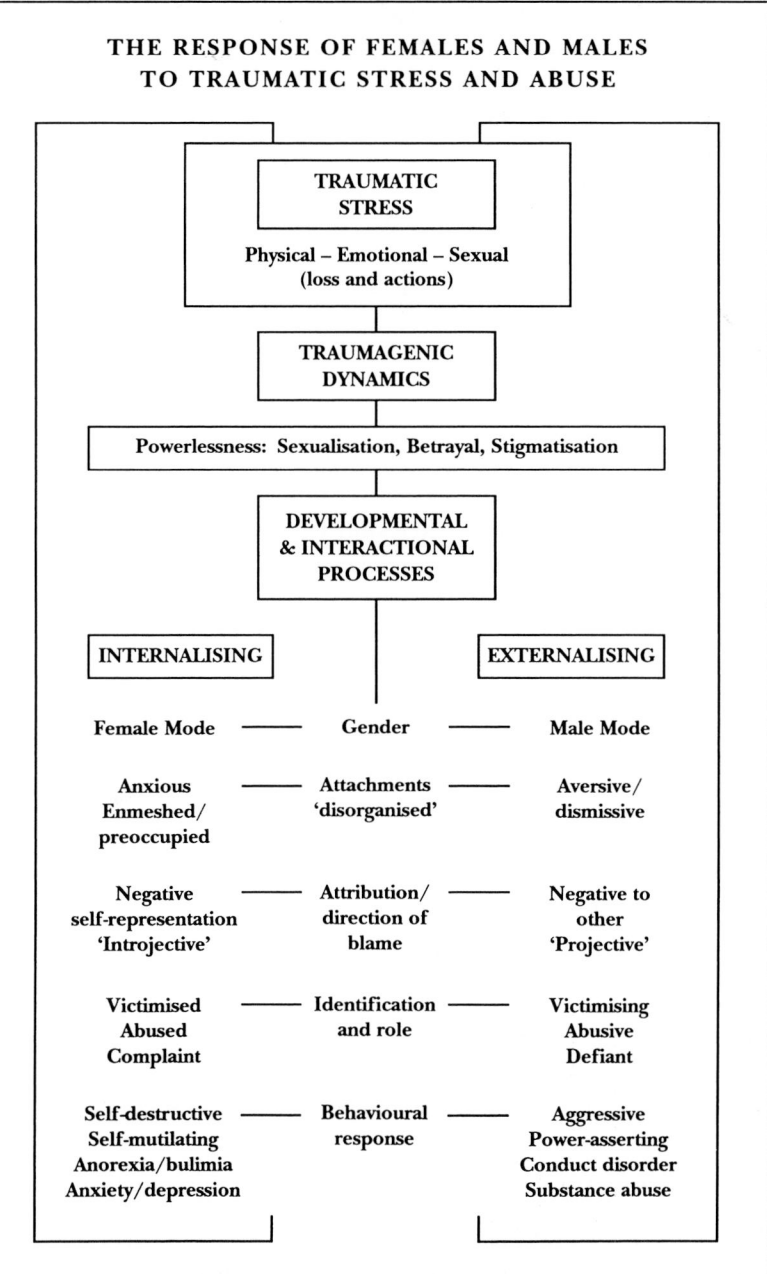

THE RESPONSE OF FEMALES AND MALES
TO TRAUMATIC STRESS AND ABUSE

**TRAUMATIC
STRESS**

Physical – Emotional – Sexual
(loss and actions)

**TRAUMAGENIC
DYNAMICS**

Powerlessness: Sexualisation, Betrayal, Stigmatisation

**DEVELOPMENTAL
& INTERACTIONAL
PROCESSES**

INTERNALISING   EXTERNALISING

Female Mode ——— Gender ——— Male Mode

Anxious ——— Attachments ——— Aversive/
Enmeshed/ 'disorganised'   dismissive
preoccupied

Negative ——— Attribution/ ——— Negative to
self-representation direction of   other
'Introjective'   blame   'Projective'

Victimised ——— Identification ——— Victimising
Abused   and role   Abusive
Complaint   Defiant

Self-destructive ——— Behavioural ——— Aggressive
Self-mutilating   response   Power-asserting
Anorexia/bulimia   Conduct disorder
Anxiety/depression   Substance abuse

Figure 6

83

if there is violence between the parents, if they have suffered disruptions of care and have been rejected by their family. An attitude of grievance is more likely to occur under these circumstances with the adoption of an abusive role in turn (*Bentovim, 1991*).

Research with both young people and adults, who have been sexually abused in childhood, indicate that being subject to penetration is a significantly traumatic effect which persists without adequate treatment even when emotional support has been offered to the child or young person (*Mullen et al, 1988*).

Poor self-esteem, self injurious behaviour and sexual abuse

One of the most worrying responses in older girls particularly those who have been abused are major depressive symptoms, poor self esteem and self worth, and self injurious behaviour. There may be overdosing, wrist slashing, anorectic responses, re-enactment of abusive experiences, and gaining relief through hurt, suicidal attempts of self starvation (*Bentovim et al, 1988*) and even 'total refusal syndromes' – withdrawal, refusal to eat, talk or walk (*Lask et al, 1991*).

Another element which comes into the process of sexual abuse is the sense of betrayal and stigmatisation which children feel as a result of the threats, secrecy and self-justifying attitude of the abuser. Guilt and a low opinion of oneself, which may lead to drug and alcohol abuse, promiscuous seeking of redeeming relationships, and clinging to unstable partners can all be responses to the victimisation process.

There may be major dissociation and repression of traumatic responses until later stages of development, when there can be profound effects on later sexual adjustment with avoidance and frozen responses, major problems in parenting and child birth and child care, and a vulner-ability to longer term depression and anxiety (*Mullen et al, 1988*).

Protective factors in sexual abuse

Children will not all suffer the same long term effects. One of the more important factors which dictates the extent of significant harm is how much support the child receives from family members after a disclosure is made. A mother's belief in her child's statement concerning abuse reduces the ill effects on the child. Children feel less depressed and feel better abut themselves when they know that they are believed and supported by the parent who should be most supportive. Paradoxically therefore in sexual abuse, the effects of abuse and the depth of harm depends both on the extent of abuse and the ability of the parent to respond with support and belief once that abuse has been disclosed (*Monck et al, 1996*).

Friedrich (*1990*) stresses the importance of a comprehensive assessment of both the child and the family, which looks at the pre- as well as the post-abuse functioning. He draws on the work of Rutter (*1983*) to identify the resilience and coping abilities of some children which may help to minimise some of the effects of sexual abuse.

Social-cognitive effects in significant harm

Many of the areas of abuse and failure of care described here can have major effects on the social-cognitive development of the individual. This may come about through the child having a particular role attributed to him, for example, being 'the bad one'. Children may identify themselves as having been responsible for their own abuse, for example, by provoking punitive responses. The sexually abused child's pre-occupations, flashbacks and poor self esteem can be pervasive, so that traumatic acts organise their cognitive reality and there may be failures in academic settings, failings of motivation, willingness to follow directions and poor self control (*Lynch & Roberts, 1982*).

Being in contact with confusing moral standards within the family has major effects on moral and societal knowledge, and the rules that govern interpersonal conduct. With such an impact on interpersonal relationships, particularly peer relationships, there are difficulties in being able to form confiding relationships and to develop intimate contacts in later life. There may be continuing confusion about the intentions of others – just as the neglected child may perceive friendly approaches as hostile, the physically abused may feel neutral responses to be hostile, the sexually abused may feel ordinary affection to be sexual approaches.

Conclusion

Significant harm can have major long term effects on all aspects of the child's development and functioning, behavioural, social-emotional, social cognitive and cognitive, as well as on physical development, growth and well being. It is not only the stressful events of abuse which are harmful, but the family context in which they occur.

Parenting which is inadequate or abusive, causing significant harm, occurs in families who fail to achieve the usual balance between positive and negative interactions, discipline and emotional bonding. There is a process whereby the families of origin of such parents may provide a 'training ground' for interpersonal violence and reduced social competence, through exposure to stressful and traumatic life events. This means they are ill prepared for the stresses of parenting, and their adaptation means that the child is seen as the cause of anger, frustrations and arousal. Abusive patterns – physical, emotional and sexual – are triggered and these become part of the inflexible maladaptive breakdown state of the family.

There are mitigating and relieving factors; not all abused children go on to become abusing adults, not all abusive parents continue their aversive interactions with their children. Recognition of families at risk – parents and children, in the earliest processes of developing abusive patterns is essential in order to break the cycle of abuse and prevent damaging processes taking root.

Bibliography

Aber, J.L., Allen, J.P., Carlson, V., Cicchetti, D. (1989). The effects of maltreatment on development during early childhood: recent studies and their theoretical, clinical and policy implications. In Cicchetti, D., Carlson, V. (Eds.) *Child Maltreatment: Theory and Research on the Causes and Consequences of Child Abuse and Neglect.* New York: Cambridge University Press.

Ainsworth, M. (1980). Attachment and Child Abuse. In Gerbner, G., Ross, C.J., Zigler, E. (Eds.) *Child abuse: An agenda for action.* Oxford University Press.

Barnett, D., Ganiban, J., Cicchetti, D. (1992). *Temperament and behaviour of youngsters with disorganised attachments: a longitudinal study presented at the 'International Conference on Infant Studies'.* Miami. April.

Bentovim, A., Elton, A., Hildebrand, J., Tranter, M., Vizard, E. (1988). *Sexual Abuse Within the Family*. Bristol: John Wright.

Bentovim, A., Kinston, W. (1991). Focal Family Therapy – joining systems theory with psychodynamic understanding. In Gurman, A., Kniskern, D. (Eds.) *Handbook for Family Therapy, Vol. 11*. New York: Basic Books.

Bentovim, A. (1991). Clinical work with families in which sexual abuse has occurred. In Hollin, C.R., Howells, K. (Eds.) *Clinical Approaches to Sex Offenders and Their Victims*. Chichester: Wiley.

Bentovim, A. (1992). *Trauma Organised Systems: Physical and Sexual Abuse in Families*. London: Karnac.

Bools, C.N., Neale, B.A., Meadow, S.R. (1991). *Co-morbidity associated with fabricated illness (Munchausen Syndrome by Proxy)*. Archives of Disease in Childhood.

Carlson, V., Cicchetti, D., Barnett, D., Braunwald, K. (1989). Disorganised/disorientated attachment relationships in maltreated infants. *Developmental Psychology*, **25**: 525–531.

Cicchetti, D., Toth, S.L. (1995). A developmental psychopathology perspective on child abuse and neglect. *Journal of the American Academy of Child and Adolescent Psychiatrist*, **34**: 541–565.

Crittenden, P.N., Bonvillian, J.D. (1984). The relationship between maternal risk status and maternal sensitivity. *American Journal of Orthopsychiatry*, **54**: 250–262.

Crittenden, P. (1988). Family and dyadic patterns of functioning in maltreating families. In Browne, K., Davies, C., Stratten, P. (Eds.) *Early Prediction and Prevention of Child Abuse*. Chichester: John Wiley.

Eckenrode, J., Laird, M., Doris, J. (1993). School performance and disciplinary problems amongst abused and neglected children. *Development Psychology*, **29**: 53–62.

Egeland, B., Sroufe, A. (1981). Attachment of early maltreatment. *Child Development*, **53**: 44–52.

Erickson, M., Egeland, B., Pianta, R. (1989). The effects of maltreatment on the development of young children. In Cicchetti, D., Carlson, V. (Eds.) *Child Maltreatment: Theory and Research on the Causes and Consequences of Child Abuse and Neglect*. New York: Cambridge University Press. pp647–684.

Finkelhor, D. (1987). The trauma of child sexual abuse: Two models. *Journal of Interpersonal Violence*, **2**: 348–366.

Friedrich, W.B. (1990). *Psychotherapy of sexually abused children and their families*. N.Y.: Norton.

Gaensbauer, T., Sands, K. (1979). Distorted affective communication in abused/neglected infants and their potential impact on caretakers. *Journal of the American Academy of Child Psychiatry*, **18**: 236–250.

Garbarino, J. (1978). The elusive 'crime' of emotional abuse. *Child Abuse and Neglect*, **2**: 89–99.

Garland, C. (1991). External disasters and the internal world: An approach to understanding survivors. In Holmes, J. (Ed.) *Handbook of Psychotherapy for Psychiatrists*. London: Churchill Livingston.

Gelles, R.J., Strauss, M.A. (1979). Determinants of violence in the family: Toward a theoretical integration. In Burr, W.R., Hill, R., Nye, F.I., Reiss, I.L. (Eds.) *Contemporary Theories about the Family*. New York: Free Press.

George, C., Main, M. (1979). Social interactions of young abused children: Approach, avoidance and aggression. *Child Development*, **50**: 306–318.

Glaser, D. (1995). Emotionally abusive experiences. In Reder, P., Lucy, C. (Eds.) *Assessment of parenting, psychiatric and psychological contributions*. London: Routledge.

Gray, J., Bentovim, A. (1996). The Induced Illness Syndrome. A series of 41 children from 37 families identified at Great Ormond Street Hospital for Children. *Journal of Child Abuse and Neglect*, **30**: 655–673.

Herrenkohl, E.C., Herrenkohl, R.C., Toedter, L., Yanushefsk, A.N. (1984). Parent child interactions in abusive and non-abusive families. *Journal of the American Academy of Child Psychiatry*, **23**: 64ˋ–648.

Kinston, W., Loader, P., Miller, L. (1987). Quantifying the clinical assessment of family health. *Journal of Marital and Family Therapy*, **13**: 49–67.

LaRose, L., Wolfe, D. (1987). Psychological characteristics of parents who abuse or neglect their children. In Lehey, B.B., Kazdin, A.E. (Eds.) *Advances in Clinical Child Psychology (Vol X)*, New York: Plenum.

Lask, B., Britten, C., Kroll, L., Magagna, J., Tranter, M., (1991). Children with pervasive refusal. *Archives of Disease in Childhood*, **66**: 866–869.

Lipsett, L. (1983). Stress in infancy: Towards understanding the origins of sleeping behaviour. In Garmezy, N., Rutter, M. (Eds.) *Stress, Coping and Development in Children*. New York: McGraw-Hill.

Lynch, M., Roberts, J. (1982). *Consequences of child abuse*. London: Academic Press.

Maccoby, E.E., Martin, J.A. (1983). Socialisation in the context of the family: Parent/child interaction. In Hetherington, E.M. (Ed.) *Handbook of Child Psychology* (Vol IV, 101-1-1).

McCleer, S., Deblinger, E., Atkins, M., Foa, E., Ralphe, D. (1988). Post Traumatic Disorder in sexually abused children. *Journal American Academy of Child and Adolescent Psychiatry*, **27**: 650–654.

Meadow, R. (1982). Munchausen Syndrome by Proxy and Pseudo-epilepsy. *Archives of Diseases in Childhood*, **57**: 811–812.

Monck, E., Bentovim, A., Goodall, G., Hyde, C., Lwin, R., Sharland, S. (1996). *Child Sexual Abuse: A descriptive treatment study*. HMSO.

Mrazek, D.A., Mrazek, P., Klinnert, M. (1995). *Clinical Assessment of Parenting of American Academy Child & Adolescent Psychiatry*, **34**: 272–282.

Mueller, E., Silverman, M. (1989). Peer relations in maltreated children. In Cicchetti, D., Carlson, V. (Eds.) *Child Maltreatment: Theory and Research on the Causes and Consequences of Child Abuse and Neglect*. New York: Cambridge University Press. 529–578.

Mullens, P.E., Romans-Clarkson, S., Walton, D.A., Herbison, G.P. (1988). Impact of sexual and physical abuse on women's mental health. *Lancet*, **1648**: 841–845.

Murray, L. (1991). *The effects of maternal depression on future infant development*. Presentation to European Child and Adolescent Psychiatry Conference, London.

Polansky, M.A., Chalmer, M., Buttenweiser, E., Williams, D. (1981). *Damaged Parents: An Anatomy of Child Neglect.* Chicago: University of Chicago Press.

Pynoos, R.S., Eth, S. (1985). (Eds.) *Post-traumatic Stress Disorder in Children.* Los Angeles: American Psychiatric Association.

Rogers, D., Tripp, J., Bentovim, A., Robinson, A., Berry, D., Goudling, R. (1976). Non-accidental poisoning: An extended syndrome of child abuse. *British Medical Journal,* 1: 793–796.

Rutter, M. (1966). *Children of sick parents – An environmental and psychiatric study.* London: Oxford University Press.

Rutter, M. (1983). Stress, coping and development: Some issues and some questions. In Garmezy, N., Rutter, M. (Eds.) *Stress, Coping and Development in Children.* New York: McGraw Hill.

Skuse, D. (1991). The relationship between deprivation, physical growth and the impaired development of language. In *Specific Speech and Language Disorders in Children.* London: Whurr. In Press.

Skuse, D. (1993). Epidemiological and definitional issues in failure to thrive. In Wollston, J. (Ed.) *Child and Adolescent Psychiatric Clinics North America.* pp37–59. Philadelphia: Saunders.

Southall, D.P., Stebbens, V.A., Rees, S.V., Lang, M.H., Warner, J.0. (1987). Apnoeic episodes induced by smothering: two cases identified by covert video surveillance. *British Medical Journal,* **294**: 1637–1641.

Spinetta, J.J., Rigler, G. (1972). The child abusing parent: A psychological review. *Psychological Bulletin,* **77**: 296–304.

Sylva, K. (1994). School influences on children's development. *Journal of Child Psychology and Psychiatry,* **35**: 135–170.

Terr, L. (1991). Child Trauma: An outline and overview. *American Journal of Psychiatry,* **148**: 10–20.

Wolfe, D.A. (1987). *Child Abuse. Implications for Child Development and Psychopathology.* California: Sage.

CHAPTER FOUR:

The effectiveness of intervention

Dr David Jones

The intent of this chapter is to present information from clinical science which may help both legal decision making and clinicians who plan interventions and give evidence in Court. Under Section 31 of the Children Act the Court has to decide if a child is suffering, or may suffer from significant harm. It must also determine (*S.1*) whether to make an order or not, with the child's future welfare as the determining principle. In these considerations the Court has to take into account the Local Authority's plan to help the child and family. Will the child's welfare be enhanced by the proposed intervention?

This chapter considers what we know about the effectiveness of intervention. Can we treat children and families where abuse and neglect have occurred? We will need to know how likely it is that an individual child will be safer, and have their welfare and care improved. This information is also likely to be relevant to the making of supervision orders with accompanying conditions, or to their variation and discharge if changes are sought.

In presenting information from the clinical literature I will avoid the concept of individual dangerousness. Instead I will attempt to consider relevant environmental and personal variables, and their inter-relationships both now and historically. This is necessary because child abuse and neglect has a multi-faceted causation and involves children and their adult carers as well as the family and cultural context in its web. Hence unitary consideration of one person's potential for danger, without appropriate historical and contextual information is relatively valueless.

Studies of families where children have been abused or neglected reveal a proportion who do not respond to the intervention of professionals. Those who work with such families know that some cannot change sufficiently to become safe enough for the child to continue to live there (*1987*). Equally a proportion change and provide adequate environments for safe child rearing. If this were not the case, all abuse by parents should be sufficient cause for permanent separation of child and parent. In between these extremes practitioners take risks when reuniting (rehabilitating) children and parents.

Practitioners have a considerable body of clinical and research literature available to them, which has examined the outcome of intervention. The following sections summarise our knowledge about the outcome of intervention in child abuse cases, the characteristics of success and failure cases, professional contributions to the success or otherwise of intervention and, finally, discuss the practical implications of all this for our work.

I. Outcome of interventions

a. Methodological aspects

Methodological difficulties have bedevilled child abuse research (*Blythe, 1983; Gough 1993; Smith et al, 1984; Widom, 1988*) thereby lowering confidence in research findings. These difficulties include; the definitions of abuse used, sampling bias and inadequate specificity about the nature of intervention used and outcome assessment criteria. Definitional problems include: a lack of clear criteria for inclusion in the research, whether abuse reports are accepted at face value, or scrutinised by the researchers, whether a Court finding of abuse is taken as the index of 'caseness', and whether cases are required to be corroborated legally. Clearly each approach would produce a different sample. Few of the studies have adequately distinguished between the severity of different cases so that, for example, cases of physical abuse involving multiple fractures are lumped together with mild bruising. In several studies, substantiated cases of abuse are included with 'at risk' cases, and treated as one group for the purpose of outcome evaluation. Sample size has been a problem in several studies, so that conclusions are based on very small numbers of cases. In addition, because the criteria for inclusion are not always specified, the reader is left to guess the representativeness of cases. Cases referred to medical, psychiatric, or psychological centres represent only a minority of the total number of cases of abuse and neglect in an area (*Gough, 1993*). Yet many reports have only studied special centres, presumably because such centres have a greater interest in researching their own programmes. This relative imbalance has been avoided, to an important extent, in the group of projects which were funded by the Department of Health in the late 1980s. These studied regular, locally-based services in various parts of the UK, rather than the work of specialised centres (*DH, 1995*).

The aims and objectives of the intervention are not always specified and in many studies there is a lack of detail describing exactly what was done, by whom and over what time period. Sometimes it is not clear whether all cases receive the same intervention. Usually, in the multi-component intervention programmes, cases receive varied amounts of the assorted intervention strategies on offer.

A greater emphasis has been placed on outcome measures. Unfortunately outcome measures with such a varied sample of people and interventions can be misleading. Researchers have been criticised for failure to use objective measurements of outcome by employing independent observers. In some studies the instruments used have lacked sensitivity and relevance to the aims of treatment. Gough (*1993*) makes a well argued case for a shift in emphasis of research strategies towards fully describing the process of intervention, or alternatively focusing on one specific aspect of intervention without attempting to do an outcome study on multi-component large projects, which he deems an impossible task.

The most important outcome variable when assessing efficacy must be the child's condition, but this is often omitted. Important aspects of child health for study include measures of child safety, re-abuse, development, growth and health. Few studies have examined changes in the interaction between parents and children attributable to the intervention (*Wolfe and Bourdeau, 1987*). There has also been criticism of the statistical methods used to determine the contribution of different elements of a case to eventual outcome (*Briere, 1988a*).

Despite these difficulties, much high quality research has been conducted. As far as practicable, the summaries which follow below have drawn upon those studies which have avoided these major difficulties. Where methodological problems do exist, attention is drawn to this in the text so that the reader can exercise due caution in accepting the findings.

b. Re-abuse

In a significant proportion of cases children are re-abused after intervention or treatment has begun. Despite the fact that re-abuse is a key outcome variable, the methods used to assess its frequency have varied from study to study, making comparisons difficult. For example Taw (*1979*) examined social services case records and revealed documentation of re-abuse which was not reflected in official figures and records. Lynch and Roberts (*1982*) found that 20% of the children in their study had been re-abused. To discover this, they searched hospital admission records, local authority social services records and individually followed up each of their cases.

Other studies have been less exhaustive in their search for evidence of re-abuse. Additionally the length of time over which re-abuse rates are reported has varied from study to study. A further problem has been the fact that re-abuse can mean anything from a slight bruise to a life threatening injury, and very few studies have discriminated between the seriousness of re-abuse (even if they have distinguished between the seriousness of the original injury). From a clinician's perspective, a re-abuse incident involving slight bruising in an older child is significantly different from skull fracture in an infant. A further fundamental problem has been that re-abuse rates have been quoted for whole samples comprising mixed cases of abuse and neglect (*Oates and Bross, 1995*). However, important issues for clinicians include the timing of re-abuse in relation to reunification attempts, and whether re-abuse occurs by the original abuser or another person. Naturally, those treatment programmes which place emphasis on child placement out of home show lower rates of re-abuse.

The four American demonstration projects (*Cohn and Daro, 1987*) and the description of Project 12 Ways (*Lutzker & Rice, 1984*) are useful sources to determine the frequency of re-abuse, as their cases samples are large. Lutzker and Rice (*1984*) compared the re-abuse rate of 352 families who had received services over a five year period with 358 comparable families who were not in their special project. Their re-abuse rate was 21.3%, versus 28.5% for the comparison families, a statistically significant difference. However the re-abuse rates in index families increased over the five years, suggesting that improvement was not maintained. Additionally there was a possible bias in the project selection criteria, with more motivated families entering the project.

In the first U.S. national demonstration project there was a 30% re-abuse rate (*see Cohn & Daro, 1987*). The strongest predictor of recidivism was the initial severity of abuse. They compared eleven different programmes and found that the lowest recidivism rates were in the programmes with the greatest proportions of highly trained workers.

Practitioners and Courts are frequently faced with the more severe end of the spectrum of abuse and with weighing up the safety and prospects of an intervention plan. Corby's (*1987*) study of twenty five such cases gives some insight into the expected rate of re-abuse in such a situation, when cases were provided with standard social case work. Seven of the twenty five children were re-abused (28%). Hensey et al (*1983*) studied moderately severe cases of abuse or neglect and found that in the half who were returned home from foster care the re-abuse rate was 20%. However in this study the nature of the intervention was variable. Cohn and Daro (*1987*) point out that early re-abuse did not always correlate with the final outcome of the case for the child and/or parents, suggesting their definition of re-abuse was quite wide, as serious re-abuse would almost certainly have led to child and parent separation.

Farmer (*1996*) reported on family reunification in a sample of 172 physically abused and neglected children who had been received into care in order to protect them from harm. 25% of those who were returned to their families were re-abused; but not always in the immediate period following return home. Levy at al (*1995*) found that the original type of maltreatment did not predict the variety of re-abuse in the 17% of their sample where this occurred, during their five year follow up period. Neglect was the commonest type of recurrence, however.

Reported re-abuse rates within the field of sexual abuse are more difficult to interpret in view of the greater secrecy surrounding sexual abuse. Low rates of re-abuse in incest offenders were reported by Gibbens et al (*1978*), but in this study the offender was often removed from the family in prison, making the comparison with family treatment programmes difficult. Kroth's (*1979*) assessment of Giaretto's programme reported a low re-abuse rate of 0.6%. However, follow-up was short and the rate determined by parent or therapist report, not by children or independent data. By contrast the re-abuse rate in the Great Ormond Street programme was 16% with a further 15% being subject to concern by the researchers (*Bentovim et al, 1988*). In the large demonstration projects (*Cohn & Daro, 1987*) the likelihood of future maltreatment, was less in the sexual abuse treatment projects, compared with those serving child neglect problems. However, these assessments were made by the therapists and cannot be taken as independent judgements.

Summary: Re-abuse following intervention occurs to a significant minority of children. It is important to examine the severity and the context to see if such re-abuse is truly the 'failure' which it appears at first sight. Nonetheless, despite being a crude index of outcome, it is especially relevant when making decisions in severe abuse cases, where re-abuse could mean a fatality. It must be noted that in the UK, child abuse fatalities have occurred in families where services were already being provided, often because of existing concerns about abuse and neglect. Yet despite this input, fatalities have occurred (*DH, 1991*).

c. Change during treatment

Examining re-abuse rates has limitations when considering the outcome of intervention. Hence, many studies have tried to examine the extent to which change occurs during intervention. Unfortunately a wide range of dimensions of change have been employed with surprisingly little attention paid to outcomes tapping the quality of life for the abused child. It seems surprising that in the field of child abuse treatment, this has not been the central measure, but many studies have dwelt on changes in attitude, belief and knowledge in the parents. The obvious criticism to be levelled at such studies is: what good is a change in such parental factors if it does not result in a) changed behaviour towards the child and b) a better outcome as far as the child is concerned? Studies assessing parental change will only be referred to here if they are linked with child outcome measures, otherwise they are of limited relevance to child abuse treatment planning. As already noted, major methodological problems sometimes affect the strength of the conclusions which can be drawn. Direct comparisons between studies are not necessarily valid, in view of the great variety of designs used. In an attempt to group studies, the large scale studies are considered first, then those conducted in specialised units, followed by those which have focused on more specific research questions within an overall treatment approach.

i. Large scale studies

The demonstration projects showed improvements in the children's developmental status, social and emotional development during the course of treatment (*Cohn & Daro, 1987*). Interestingly the later study (*study 4*) demonstrated gains for over 70% of the young children and adolescents in all functional areas during treatment. This was despite the fact that in that study there were more cases of serious abuse than in the earlier projects. Parents also showed improvements in behaviour and attitude. In approximately half of the cases future abuse was considered unlikely. The provision of group counselling and educational and skill development classes showed a significant relationship to successful outcome. The addition of volunteers to the professional treatment package also improved outcome. As in other studies, (*e.g. Famularo et al, 1989; Smith & Rachman, 1984*) many families refused to co-operate and, not surprisingly, those who dropped out did not do so well as those remaining in treatment longer than six months (*Cohn & Daro, 1987*). Interestingly, the sub-group of clients who stayed longer than eighteen months did less well (possibly because they included intractable cases where persistence produced little change despite much effort). Better results were achieved by the first demonstration project and by Project 12 ways, where staff made efforts to engage reluctant clients through visits, phone calls and flexible working patterns, including home visits (*Cohn, 1979; Cohn & Daro, 1987; Lutzker & Rice, 1984*).

ii. Detailed process studies

These studies have carefully described the process of decision making and the type of case management. Studies of the process whereby typical child protection cases are managed have been less numerous (*see Gough, 1993 at Chapter 5*). Gough et al (*1987*) studied all pre-school cases which were registered in one area of Scotland. They found that the majority of cases were managed by social workers without much input from health or other agencies. The focus of work was on parenting skills, not on the needs of the child. A very wide variety of predicaments became included in the child abuse 'net'. Poverty and families with marginal coping skills were the commonest cases registered, compared with abuse. To measure outcome in the face of such diversity was therefore very difficult. Nevertheless over half the cases either improved or remained the same. Cases which could be broadly described as neglect did relatively worse than others.

Another approach is to study the management of particular sorts of cases in detail. Corby (*1987*) selected 25 cases from the moderate to severe end of the spectrum of child protection cases. He found great variety in the types of intervention offered, and emphasised the difficulty involved with oversimplifying the concept of outcome.

iii. Specialised centre programmes

There have been several descriptions of specialised programmes which have reported their success or otherwise at achieving change. Elizabeth Elmer and colleagues (*1986*) report on their results with an intensive programme of treatment, residential assessment, stimulation and parent teaching and modelling, for 'last chance' cases referred by the Courts. They showed significant improvements so far as the children were concerned: height, weight and interaction with their adult carers all improved. However only three of the thirty one children remained at home; the remainder were placed in foster care (*Elmer et al, 1986*). Lynch and Roberts (*1982*) report that nine out of thirty nine children (23%) they studied did well over the follow up period. The remainder had continuing problems to varying degrees. In thirteen of the thirty three children who were not in care, but still at home, child care was poor. These children frequently had accompanying medical, psychological and school problems.

iv. Focused treatments

These include most of the behavioural modification programmes as well as a small number of studies which have used other treatment modalities. In general, the outcome assessment has not encompassed the whole process of child and family change. Rather, it has focused on one aspect of change in order to see whether the specific aims of treatment have been met. For example, Nicol et al (*1988*) compared a focused case work approach based on Paterson's social learning theory, and aimed at parent child interactions, with structured play therapy for the child alone. The groups were well matched and both sets of families continued to have normal social case work and child protection services. There was a high drop out rate in both groups, but greater improvement was seen in the focused case work regime: this led to a specific reduction in coercive and negative behaviour.

Kitchur and Bell (*1989*) described their group treatment for pre-adolescent, sexually abused girls, utilising self esteem and child behaviour outcome measures and demonstrated the benefit of the group in both these dimensions, in a methodologically sound study. Deblinger et al (*1990*) studied a group of children treated with a cognitive behavioural programme specifically designed for child victims of sexual abuse. Using standardised measures they demonstrated significant improvement in both the child and their non offending parent. Studies such as these which focus on a specific aspect of an overall treatment plan for abused children and families are of great value to practitioners who are developing treatment plans.

Cohen and Mannarino have described a programme of cognitive behaviour therapy for sexually abused pre-school children, comparing it with non-directive supportive therapy, demonstrating superior results from the cognitive therapy approach, which was maintained at a follow up period (*Cohen and Mannarino, 1997*). Their intervention was highly structured, time limited and focused on particular target symptoms such as sexually inappropriate behaviours, aggression, sadness, as well as regressive behaviours.

One special feature of this study was that the intervention specifically addressed the experience of having been sexually abused, with the children. The authors demonstrate the importance of doing this, to the extent that such direct work was one important component of their intervention. As they acknowledge, however, they did not independently evaluate this particular component from the other components employed in their cognitive behaviour treatment programme. They placed the same caveat upon the value of the parallel intervention which they did with the non-offending parent. However, neither of these two important components of treatment appeared to prevent the beneficial impact of cognitive behaviour therapy being demonstrated, and this, combined with the fact that the process observations of the study strongly supported the value of both these two elements of the intervention are strongly persuasive that the focus on the children's experience, and the work with non abusive parents were important components.

Summary: Change, following child maltreatment is possible, though in the main, parental change has been more possible to demonstrate than beneficial child outcomes. Considerable imagination and outreach towards families, with the intention of working in partnership, has been demonstrated to be of major importance in achieving good outcomes. At the same time it is shown that there is little value in persisting with reluctant families after an initial trial period of intervention – some families were simply unreachable. Child neglect has proved especially resistant to change. Despite the best efforts, child care outcomes remain poor in a substantial minority. Focused treatment approaches, which target specific symptoms in the child resulting from maltreatment and neglect, show the most promise in more recent studies. Focused approaches, and especially those involving cognitive behavioural techniques have shown particular promise.

In the field of sexual abuse, parallel work with child victims themselves and their non-offending parents or carers, has proved valuable (*Finkelhor & Berliner, 1995; Jones, 1996*). It is possible that treatments which are able to focus on the abuse experience are particularly important so far as improving child outcomes is concerned.

II. Characteristics of successful and failure cases

This section of the paper considers those studies which have described the characteristics of children and/or families where intervention was successful or, alternatively, unsuccessful. Studies concentrating on this aspect of outcome have identified several characteristics which describe families falling into these two extremes of the spectrum of outcome. Studies have not distinguished the relative weight of each characteristic, so far, and so to state which factors are the most important is not yet possible. Ultimately, the weighting of different factors in an individual case must remain a clinical decision.

A further problem is that there is circularity of reasoning involved with these studies. That is, the decision is made by practitioners not to proceed with treatment because of certain factors which are, in turn, listed as the characteristics of 'untreatable' cases. Thus the studies described below are perhaps best considered as descriptions of what was current practice in the few years prior to their publication date.

The studies which have been conducted do have several other methodological problems, too. One issue is that there has been a lack of distinction between cases where parents refuse to even start treatment, those who engage initially but then do not cooperate later, and finally those who start and cooperate but cannot change enough or sufficiently quickly for their child's development. These are vital distinctions, which are not always clear in the studies. This issue is further complicated by the unrepresentativeness of cases. As Gough (*1993*) points out, studies less commonly describe all cases in an area, concentrating instead on specialised treatment centres which select cases for inclusion. Despite these cautions some of the findings from selected studies will now be discussed.

Treatment failure

Early studies describing treatment failures concentrated on personality attributes or psychiatric descriptions of the parents (*Kempe and Kempe, 1978; Gabinet, 1983; Green et al, 1981*). These studies were not able to relate such parental qualities to severity or type of initial abuse, parent-child interaction, family functioning, quality and type of treatment or indeed child variables. Despite these methodological reservations, their descriptions of intervention and failures show some common threads. The Kempes (1978) pointed to seven groups of parents who commonly proved untreatable: aggressive psychopaths, parents with delusions that involve their child, cruel sadistic parents who painfully abuse their children with pre-meditation, extreme fanatics, drug and substance abusers, mentally handicapped parents, and families with a history of prior serious injury or child abuse death. Gabinet (1983) found that parents who are sociopaths, addicts, severely inadequate personalities, mentally handicapped combined with a personality disorder and 'focal' abusers were over represented in her treatment failure cases (focal abusers were those who did not have problems in areas other than abusing their children, and were similar to some of the Kempes' fanatics, who were outwardly respectable yet parented their children abusively). In Gabinet's study severely mentally handicapped or psychotic parents were not accepted for treatment. However, the other major group in her study who proved untreatable were those who refused treatment in the first place.

Green et al (1981) found that treatment failures were more likely to have the following characteristics: to have repeatedly abused their child prior to discovery, to be involuntarily in treatment, to have ended treatment prematurely against advice, to deny that they had abused their child, to have a history of serious abuse in childhood themselves, to have had premature expectations of their child and to show an impaired ability to relate to other adults. In a later study of forty five abusive parents from the same treatment centre, Ferleger et al (1988) found that lack of compliance by parents was the best indicator of later re-abuse (which occurred in 40% of their sample). Famularo et al (1988) looked at parental compliance in more detail and discovered that it was lower in those cases involving physical abuse and sexual abuse, than in neglect, and was substantially reduced if there was parental substance abuse.

One of the biggest problems facing those providing intervention services in abuse and neglect is that of overcoming high refusal rates and parental denial that a problem exists at all. One controversial aspect of this is the extent to which civil court orders help to motivate reluctant parents where abuse has been substantiated in courts. Wolfe et al's (*1980*) randomised prospective trial of court order versus voluntary treatment provided some preliminary evidence that the court ordered group did better than the voluntary. This was despite the fact that the court ordered group tended to contain cases of greater severity. In a similar vein Irueste-Montes and Montes (*1988*) looked at thirty five court ordered cases of abuse and neglect compared with thirty who entered treatment voluntarily. There was a high drop out rate from both groups and once again the court ordered group seemed to contain the more serious cases of abuse. Their outcome measures included a careful observation of the quality of interactions between parent and child. Both groups improved to an equal degree in terms of parent/child interactions. The authors interpret the results as indicating that court orders do not act as an obstruction to effective intervention. Bearing in mind that in both studies the Court ordered group contained more serious cases, yet still did as well or better than the voluntary, these studies support the clinical impression that the Court's structure and direction helps to improve outcome.

In the UK, Dale et al (*1986*) described the experience of the NSPCC Special Unit in Rochdale, working with the serious end of the spectrum of child abuse cases; they had twenty six families in all. Their intervention consisted of a three to four month intensive assessment of the capacity for change, followed by continuing rehabilitative efforts over the next two years. 55% of the children were included in their 'sustained rehabilitation' group (i.e. the group with whom they continued rehabilitative efforts after the end of the intensive assessment period). They had therefore weeded out the families who would not comply with their treatment programme and those with whom rehabilitation was attempted but proved unsafe or not possible. In the 55% who remained in their 'sustained rehabilitation' group there was no re-abuse. Independent outcome measures were not employed, but their study contains a wealth of valuable detail about clinical decision making and the range of their work with children and families.

The 'sustained rehabilitation' group were characterised by parents who took greater responsibility for the abuse caused; showed an awareness of difficulties in the spousal relationship and their parenting ability; and demonstrated a willingness to tackle the difficulties. In addition the children demonstrated a wish, either directly or indirectly, to return home. By contrast, in the group where permanent separation, voluntary or otherwise, was the end result, the parents did not take responsibility for the abuse caused, frequently failed to engage with the therapeutic staff, and themselves tended to have a history of severe abuse and/or deprivation in their own childhoods, which they were unprepared to tackle during therapeutic work. With regard to their own adult partnership, these parents lacked awareness of difficulties or there was continuing violence between them. In addition they found that the permanent separation group were associated with the more serious injuries. By 'more serious' they include more extreme forms of violence and resultant injury, together with those where there was premeditation or sadism involved (e.g. burning, scalding). This association between outcome and seriousness was not found by the Denver Circle House Group (*McBogg et al, 1979*) or the Park Hospital Group (*Lynch and Roberts, 1982*). However, definitions of seriousness were not necessarily comparable. Furthermore, both sample size and range of seriousness makes comparison unreliable.

The final end point of decision making in the American Civil Courts is that of the termination of parental rights, after a treatment plan has been tried and failed. Schetky et al (*1979*) report their experience when assessing such families prior to termination of parental rights hearings. They report that parental lack of empathy, viewing the child as a possession, parental history of abuse in childhood with current low self esteem, poor judgement and impulsivity, maternal psychosis and paternal personality disorders (usually sociopathy) were the most common features among those parents whose rights were terminated. The authors add that many of these parents refused any form of help or treatment in the first place.

Does the type or severity of abuse correlate with treatment outcome? These are more complex issues than appear at first sight. The discrimination between types of abuse has been poorly distinguished in most studies. Practitioners tend to select what they perceive as the most prominent category when filling out statistical returns, frequently ignoring mixed categories or coding the abuse type. A further complication is that abuse type itself is an administrative label, to a large degree, and not an accurate description for all the abuses and neglects befalling an individual child.

As clinicians, we have stressed the need for a more complete understanding of the range of abuse and neglect and parenting qualities in any individual abuse case (*Bentovim, 1990; Jones, 1991 and 1997; Jones & Alexander, 1987*). Does neglect or emotional abuse accompany the abuse, and if so to what extent? Claussen and Crittenden (*1991*) underlined the concerns of clinicians that underlying emotional abuse and neglect may be as important, if not more so, than the officially categorised abuse type, in terms of eventual outcome for the child. None of the treatment outcome studies have documented adequately the full range of abuse and neglect present in individual cases, let alone related this to outcome, in order to overcome such issues. Claussen & Crittenden were among the first to attempt to do so. Interestingly, they found that child outcome was unrelated to severity of original injury, whereas physical abuse coexisting with psychological maltreatment was highly correlated with outcome. Also physical abuse hardly ever occurred without concurrent psychological maltreatment. In contrast, psychological abuse did occur alone. Thus the occurrence of mixed types of abuse and severe underlying emotional abuse and neglect is highly likely to affect outcome and response to treatment.

'Severity' itself is a complex notion. It is likely to include the degree and extent of physical harm, duration and frequency of abuse. Still further factors appear to include the extent of premeditation (*Dale et al, 1986*) degree of threat and coercion (*Conte & Schuerman, 1987*) sadism (*Dale et al, 1986*) and bizarre or unusual elements, in child sexual abuse (*Briere, 1988b*). Each of these, or combinations thereof have been associated with more severe effects on the child and/or relatively greater difficulty for treatment. It must be noted that, at least in part, severity is defined by outcome and hence the issues of severity and successful outcome are partially circular constructs.

In summary then there have been variable findings with respect to type of abuse and outcome. It seems that mixed types of abuse and severe types of sexual abuse may be very resistant to treatment. Also there are few case reports of successful intervention in Munchausen syndrome by proxy, or deliberate poisoning cases. With regard to severity, although this is a complex concept, there is an association between severity of abuse and treatment outcome, in some, but not all, studies.

One interesting study attempted to examine the relative contribution of these different factors. Ferleger et al (*1988*) showed a significant interaction between re-abuse and severity of abuse, in relation to percentage of kept appointments, suggesting that the relationship between severe abuse and outcome is not a direct one, but one which involves the degree to which parents can engage with treatment efforts. This emphasises the critical position of compliance in child abuse work (*see above*).

Cases which succeed

Studies of successful families have been less numerous but are of equal relevance to practising clinicians. Lynch and Roberts (*1982*) described in detail the nine out of thirty nine children who did well in their study; they featured: uncomplicated pregnancy and birth, no prematurity, younger age (less than two years) when diagnosed, higher levels of language and intellectual abilities, absence of brain damage, and fewer subsequent placements. Conte and Scheurman (*1987*) demonstrated that, in sexual abuse cases, children who did well were more likely to have been subjected to sexual abuse which was non-penetrative, to have received the support of an adult person in the wake of discovery of abuse, and to have developed more healthy and appropriate attributions about who was responsible for their abuse.

There has been recent interest in which coping styles auger for a better outcome for those children who have been abused. It appears that active, expressive styles of coping are better than self destructive, self blaming or avoidant forms, so far as children's adjustment is concerned (*Chaffin et al, 1997; Runtz & Schallow, 1997*). However, avoidant styles may confer benefit to some children (*Chaffin et al, 1997*). In several of the studies, social support from a parent was significantly associated with these more positive coping styles (*Chaffin et al, 1997; Runtz & Schallow, 1997; Spaccarelli & Kim, 1995*).

Follow up studies of abused (*Egeland et al, 1988*) and deprived (*Rutter, 1989*) women, currently parenting their own children, have underscored the importance of corrective school experiences, non-abusive and corrective relationships with peers during childhood, having a non abusive adult partner who provides support, and therapeutic intervention as a child, as important factors, distinguishing women who parent their own offspring satisfactorily, despite their miserable childhood experiences.

Summary: We have examined a range of studies from clinical practice which are broadly linked to the extent in which they consider the characteristics of those families who did relatively well in treatment, and compared with those who did less well. Besides the valuable insights about the process of intervention and treatment services, these studies do give us some clues as to the factors which might be associated with relatively better, or alternatively worse outcome. As already noted there is a certain circularity with these studies, to the extent that if practitioners do not believe that particular types of cases are capable of being intervened with, then, of course, they will not be accepted into treatment programmes, and then they become relatively poor prospect cases, by definition. Nonetheless, the features listed below appear in more than one study describing the unsuccessful cases, lending credence to their inclusion below.

- Continuing parental denial of abuse or impairment

- Parents who refuse help or do not cooperate with professional help (clinically, refusal is seen more frequently, but not exclusively, in cases of burning, scalding, Munchausen Syndrome by Proxy (MSBP) and severe sexual abuse)

- Severe parental personality problems: antisocial, aggressive or inadequate.

- Parental mental handicap with accompanying mental illness.

- Persistent parental substance/alcohol misuse.

- Parental psychosis with delusions involving the child.

- Severe accompanying child neglect or psychological abuse (included here are cases where parents demonstrate pervasive lack of empathy for the child).

- Severe sexual abuse (involving penetration and of long duration).

- Sadistic abuse or that which includes slow, premeditated infliction of pain and suffering.

- Mixed abuse cases.

- Certain types of abuse cases, e.g. MSBP, deliberate poisoning, scalding and burns.

Identifying those cases with better prospects for success has been more difficult but some important features do emerge from the projects which have examined this.

- Those infants and children who despite abuse do not have residual disability, developmental delay or educational special needs.

- Those children subjected to less severe abuse or neglect.

- Children who have had the benefit of non-abusive or corrective relationships with peers, siblings and/or a supportive adult.

- Children who have developed more healthy and appropriate attributions about the maltreatment which they had suffered.

- Children and families who are able and willing to cooperate with helping agencies.

- Children and families who have been able to engage in therapeutic work.

- Situations where successful partnerships between professionals and family members have occurred.

- Children and families where the psychological abuse component of the maltreatment experience has been amenable to change.

The group of studies described above do give us some clues, despite methodological reservations, as to the characteristics of cases more likely to result in successful outcome for the child. In addition, they point the way toward the most useful intervention and therapeutic strategies.

III. Professional factors

The unwillingness of a significant minority of parents to comply with the professionals' management plan is a central theme in several studies (*Gabinet, 1983; Smith & Rachman, 1984*). Some families do not choose to engage at all, others seem to try but drop out of treatment early on. Not surprisingly, this group have been poorly studied as they tend to be unavailable to researchers too. But what about the professional contribution of the professional/client relationship? In general, relatively little work has examined the work of the professional system. There is a large literature describing which factors professionals take into account when making decisions (*see helpful summary by Dalgleish and Drew, 1989*), but much less interest in how professionals intervene and what consumers think about intervention.

Corby (*1987*) and Brown (*1984*) have demonstrated that how professionals intervene may be relatively more important to parents than exactly what they do. Consumers (parents) found patronising and authoritarian approaches with inadequate explanation the most difficult and negative professional responses. Both studies found that negative initial experiences influence parents future relationships with the professionals. On the other hand, parents responded warmly to empathic accessible professionals who emanated genuineness and a positive regard for them, despite the use of child protection powers. In Brown's study (*1984*) families often expressed the wish to have a different social worker from the one they were allocated, complaining that they could not get on with him/her. In general the professional response to this request is to minimise its relevance, taking it as a further demonstration of the parent's oppositionalism and lack of compliance. At present a lack of available resources make such choices a luxury. However, it should be noted that those who can afford to pay for therapeutic help are able to exercise some choice over whom they work with concerning sensitive personal issues. By contrast, social services clients are rarely permitted to exercise choice over which professional they work with (*Brown, 1984*). Increasingly, agencies have been attempting to provide choice, wherever practicable. However, this question has not been systematically explored, to date.

We studied the responses and views of a group of children and parents who had experienced a typical social services led child protection investigation of possible sexual abuse. The results were sobering (*Sharland at al, 1996*). The child's primary carer, usually the mother, experienced substantial shock, distress and mental anguish, which was frequently unrecognised by the professional. However, both mothers and the children themselves generally appreciated the professionals' work, initially. Parents appreciated being kept informed, and professional openness and honesty. Children responded to those professionals who interacted with them directly, and who responded in an age appropriate way to their children. However, one year following disclosure this picture had changed substantially, as unmet needs for help with psychological problems, in both parents and children, became more prominent. Our study indicated that the quality of professional intervention could have an effect on the trajectory of a case, tending to turn initially optimistic cases into poor outcome cases and visa versa. Unrealised expectations of professional help led to increasing disillusion among the parents. Nonetheless, parental psychiatric symptoms slowly improved over the year following disclosure. But children did not show the same levels of improvement, and a minority actually deteriorated. These results were remarkably similar to those of Berliner and Conte (*1995*) in the USA, who undertook a similar study.

Summary: Professional factors do contribute to the outcome for children and families following the recognition of child abuse and neglect. It is probable that professional factors exert an effect on outcome over and above that which is attributable to the abuse and the context within which this occurs. This is an extremely important observation with major implications for training and supervision of social work, mental health and paediatric services. It is also of particular importance because, while little can be done to alter the severity of an abusive act which has occurred, nor in many cases the miserable context within which such abuse was perpetrated, professional factors are amenable to change.

IV. Implications for practice

How can all this material be incorporated into the management of cases where there has been child abuse? Are there sufficiently robust findings from more than one study to enable us to have confidence in the research findings to date? While further research is almost always needed in such complex matters, certain lessons can already be usefully drawn and applied to help the practitioner. Initially, the task for professionals is investigation to determine whether abuse or neglect has occurred. Following this, the next stage in the assessment process, once abuse or neglect has been established, is to assess the child and family context sufficiently to be able to secure child protection. Later on, the process develops into an assessment of the likelihood of change, followed by whether such change is achieved. Looked at in this way, assessment continues throughout intervention. There is good reason to suggest that the quality of the work in the investigation phase sets the tone for subsequent intervention. Some parents may be unable to engage in any form of change at all, from the outset.

The research findings can be summarised in a table of these characteristics which have been associated with a more positive outcome, contrasted with those associated with a more negative one (*Table 1*). While no factor should be taken as a definite indicator that a particular child and family will not be amenable to treatment, or on the other hand will definitely respond, the characteristics listed may alert the practitioner to those positive or negative features about the individual case which aid planning. In the clinical situation, these various factors will need to be weighed relative to one another. It is probable that parental factors generally carry greater weight than other domains (*Kaufman and Zigler, 1989*), but greater predictive precision is not yet feasible. These case factors will now need to be considered in the light of the parents' likely compliance. Applying these research findings to the individual case will allow a prognosis to be estimated. Cases with a poorer prognosis are more likely to need comprehensive court powers to secure the child's safety. Those with a good prognosis may not require an order at all, despite perhaps the presence of significant harm. In between these extremes lie many cases where the estimated prognosis is guarded or

FACTORS INVOLVED IN SUCCESS OR FAILURE

Factors	Rehabilitation more likely to fail	Rehabilitation more likely to succeed
Abuse	Severe physical abuse inc. burns/scalds Severe failure to thrive Mixed abuse Child sexual abuse, with penetration or over long duration MSBP Sadistic abuse	Less severe forms of abuse If severe, yet compliance and lack of denial, success still possible
Child	Developmental delay with special needs Very young – requiring rapid parental change	Healthy child attributions (in child sexual abuse) Later age of onset One good corrective relationship

Parent	Personality – Antisocial
	            – Sadism
	            – Aggressive
	Lack of compliance
	Denial of problems
	Learning difficulties plus mental illness
	Substance abuse
	Paranoid psychosis
	Abuse in childhood – not recognised as a problem
		Non-abusive partner
		
		Compliance
		Acceptance of problem
		Responsibility taken
		
		Mental illness, responsive to treatment
		Healthy adaptation

Parenting & parent/child interaction	Disordered attachment Lack of empathy for child Own needs before child	Normal attachment Empathy for child Competence in some areas
Family	Pervasive family violence Power problems; poor negotiation, autonomy and expression of affect	Absence of other forms of violence Non abusive partner Capable of change Supportive, cooperative extended family

Table 1

(continued)

Factors	Rehabilitation more likely to fail	Rehabilitation more likely to succeed
Professional	Lack of resources Ineptitude	Therapeutic relationship with child Outreach to family Partnership with parents
Social setting	Social isolation Violent unsupportive neighbourhood	More local child care facilities Volunteer networks Social support

qualified. In these, some order may be necessary to provide the necessary catalyst and/or framework for continuing assessment and therapy.

Gauging parental compliance can prove difficult because the parent may be under pressure from extended family, solicitors or through personal guilt, to appear more cooperative than she or he truly feels. Under the Children Act, the wide menu of available Orders, together with the variations which can be sought (e.g. Supervision Orders, Interim Orders with directions), allow for subsequent changes to be made if parental co-operation is insufficiently sustained.

Professional factors will also need to be considered, including the availability of basic resources. From this matrix the professional can specify a process of change for the family involved. This may include any treatment provision, proposed interventions, counselling or support. If relevant, the stages which the family are expected to undergo may be specified. Increasingly, practitioners find it useful to set out the criteria for gauging whether the intervention will have been successful or otherwise, at this initial planning stage (*Jones 1991 and 1997*). Lastly, but probably all importantly, the time scale for intervention will need to be set out at the beginning. This is because the time scale will depend on the age and developmental needs of the individual child. Table 2 lists the processes which may be involved in estimating the prospects for a change after a comprehensive assessment has been undertaken. In some cases an initial assessment will be necessary, followed by a clinical review and setting further goals for intervention, especially in complicated cases. Other cases, however, may be able to be dealt with in a single process of assessment and goal setting, followed by assessment of outcome in the future.

Table 2

Consideration when estimating prospects for change

Case and professional factors (*Table 1*)
Expected process of change (inc. treatment, counselling)
Criteria for success
Timescale for change

We can summarise the processes described above in a series of stages which the practitioner can consider and apply to the individual case. This process has been described as one of risk assessment though in many respects risk assessment is merely the description of good, methodical practice applied to 'risky' situations. Child abuse and neglect is quite clearly one such risky situation. Table 3 sets out the stages which have been identified above, which a practitioner can apply, based upon the research findings which have been reviewed in this article, to the 'risky business' in which they are engaged.

Table 3

---

1. Gather all relevant information from all domains, including positive and negative features.

2. Weight all factors, in order to define the current risk.

3. Identify those future circumstances which might increase or decrease risk (considering all domains of risk and proposed treatment strategies).

4. Assess the likelihood of successful intervention.

5. Make a prognosis, based on nos. 3 & 4, identifying the likelihood of particular outcomes occurring (risk prediction).

6. Risk management plan (who will notice changes and what will they do?)

7. When will the next review occur?

How might these assessments be conducted under the Act? It might be said that the Act's guiding principle of avoiding delay will result in insufficient time being available to conduct complex assessments. However, the menu of available orders, together with the opportunities available under the Act to bring cases back to court, should mean that even complex cases can be comprehensively assessed within a time scale which ensures that the necessary work is not compromised. The outcome of intervention can be periodically reviewed while the child's welfare is kept central. In severe abuse cases, a 'split' hearing has been found to assist therapeutic progress greatly. In these, findings of fact on the threshold criteria are made early on, with a final hearing delayed until risk assessment and some initial therapeutic work has been completed.

Conclusions

The available research can aid clinical decision making. The research on the outcome of intervention in child abuse engenders realism about the general likelihood of success. However, given that severe child abuse by a caregiver represents such a severe breakdown in parenting, it is hardly surprising that treatment results are modest. Above all, the results of these studies provide a powerful case for careful treatment planning. Such planning includes specifying the aims and objectives of intervention, the criteria for success or failure and the expected time frame, given the child's developmental status, right at the start of inter-vention. Cases take time to assess properly as well as to effect change. Intervention may need to be planned in stages. The legal umbrella necessary for each stage may prove different as the case unfolds, dependent upon progress and parental cooperativeness. Professionals working with abusing families need to appreciate the research messages in order to plan interventions effectively. Also, once professionals appreciate that success rates are modest, it becomes clear that the important 'outcome' to measure must be the welfare of the child.

In some cases hard decisions will need to be made swiftly enough to prevent the child's development being adversely affected. Family reunification is desirable, but only provided that an improved situation for the child is the paramount aim of any intervention. Wald (*1982*) proposed an outside time limit of 12 months for those families in which the child is under 3 years, and 18 months for these over 3 years, before permanent alternative arrangements for parenting are made. Professionals can be encouraged to regard effective relinquishment as an equally legitimate therapeutic goal in some cases. This position becomes perfectly acceptable, if 'success' is seen as essentially a child welfare criterion. Furthermore, in order to prevent 'burn-out' and to preserve human and financial resources, we cannot afford to keep trying relentlessly with cases where there is minimal hope of change. This constitutes a realistic acceptance of both our own and the families' limitations, preserving therapeutic optimism for the more feasible cases.

Bibliography

Bentovim, A. (1990). Family Violence: Clinical Aspects (Section VII, Chapter 8, pp543–561). In Bluglass, R., Bowden, P. (Eds.) *Principles and Practice of Forensic Psychiatry.* Edinburgh: Churchill Livingstone.

Bentovim, A., Elton, A., Hildebrand, J., Tranter, M., Vizard, E. (1988). *Child Abuse Within the Family: Assessment and Treatment.* London: John Wright.

Berliner, L., Conte, J. (1995). The effects of disclosure and intervention on sexually abused children. *Child Abuse & Neglect,* **19**: 371–384.

Blythe, B. (1983). A critique of outcome evaluation in child abuse treatment. *Child Welfare,* **62**: 325–335.

Briere, J. (1988a). Controlling for family variable in abuse effects research: a critique of the partialling approach. *J Interpers Violence,* **3**: 80–89.

Briere, J. (1988b). The long term clinical correlates of childhood sexual victimisation. *Annals of the New York Academy of Science,* **528**: 327–334.

Brown, C. (1984). *Child Abuse Parents Speaking.* Bristol: University of Bristol.

Chaffin, M., Wherry, J., Dykman, R. (1997). School aged children's coping with sexual abuse: Abuse stresses and symptoms associated with four coping strategies. *Child Abuse & Neglect,* **21**: 227–240.

Claussen, A.H., Crittenden, P.M. (1991). Physical and psychological maltreatment, relations among types of maltreatment. *Child Abuse & Neglect,* **15**: 5–18.

Cohen, J., Mannarino, A. (1997). A treatment study for sexually abused preschool children: outcome during a one year follow up. *Journal of the American Academy of Child and Adolescent Psychiatry,* **36**: 122–1235.

Cohn, A.H. (1979). Effective treatment of child abuse and neglect. *Social Work,* **24**: 513–519.

Cohn, A.H., Daro, D. (1987). Is treatment too late; what 10 years of evaluative research tells us. *Child Abuse & Neglect,* **11**: 433–442.

Conte, J. R., Schuerman, J.R. (1987). Factors associated with an increased impact of sexual abuse. *Child Abuse & Neglect,* **11**: 201–212.

Corby, B. (1987). *Working with Child Abuse.* Oxford: Oxford University Press.

Dale, P., Davies, M., Morrison, T., Waters, J. (1986). *Dangerous Families; Assessment and Treatment of Child Abuse.* London: Tavistock Publications.

Dalgleish, L., Drew, E. (1989). The relationship of child abuse indicators to the assessment of perceived risk and to the court's decision to separate. *Child Abuse & Neglect,* **13**: 491–506.

Deblinger, E., McVeer, S.V., Henry, D. (1990). Cognitive behavioural treatment for sexually abused children suffering post traumatic stress; preliminary findings. *Journal of the American Academy of Child & Adolescent Psychiatry,* **29**: 747–752.

Department of Health (1995). *Child Protection; Messages from Research.* London: HMSO.

Department of Health (1991). *Child Abuse; a study of Inquiry Reports.* London: HMSO.

Egeland, B., Jacobvitz, D., Sroufe, L.A. (1988). Breaking the cycle of abuse. *Child Development,* **59**: 1080–1088.

Elmer, E. (1986). Outcome of residential treatment for abused and high risk infants. *Child Abuse & Neglect,* **10**: 351–360.

Famularo, R., Kinscherff, R., Bunshaft, D., Spivak, Fenton, T. (1989). Parental compliance to court ordered treatment interventions in cases of child maltreatment. *Child Abuse & Neglect,* **13**: 507–514.

Farmer, E. (1996). Family Reunification with High Risk Children: Lessons from Research. *Children and Youth Services Review,* **18**: 403–424.

Ferleger, N., Glenwick, D., Gaines, R., Green, A.H., (1988). Identifying correlates of re-abuse in maltreating parents. *Child Abuse & Neglect,* **12**: 41–49.

Finkelhor, D., Berliner, L. (1995). Research on the treatment of sexually abused children: a review and recommendations. *Journal of the American Academy of Child and Adolescent Psychiatry,* **34**: 1408–1423.

Gabinet, L. (1983). Child abuse treatment failures reveal need for redefinition of the problem. *Child Abuse & Neglect,* **7**: 395–402.

Gibbens, T.C.N. Soothill, K.L., Way, C.K. (1978). Sibling and parent-child incest offenders. *British Journal of Criminology,* **18**: 40–52.

Gough, D. (1993). *Child Abuse Interventions: A Review of the Research Literature.* London: HMSO.

Gough, D.A., Boddy, F.A., Dunning, N., Stone, P.H. (1987). *A Longitudinal Study of Child Abuse in Glasgow, Volume 1.* Glasgow: Public Health Research Unit, The University of Glasgow.

Green, A.H., Power, E., Steinook, B., Gaines, R. (1981). Factors associated with successful and unsuccessful intervention with child abusive families. *Child Abuse & Neglect,* **5**: 45–52.

Hensey, O.J., Williams, J., Rosenbloom, L. (1983). Intervention in child abuse, experience in Liverpool. *Developmental Medicine and Child Neurology,* **25**: 606–611.

Irueste-Montes, A., Montes, F. (1988). Court ordered vs. voluntary treatment of abusive and neglectful parents. *Child Abuse & Neglect,* **12**: 33–39.

Jones, D.P.H. (1987). The untreatable family. *Child Abuse & Neglect,* **11**: 409–420.

Jones, D.P.H. (1991). Working with the Children Act: tasks and responsibilities of the child and adolescent psychiatrist. In Lindsey, C. (Ed.) *Proceedings of the Children Act 1989 Course.* London: Royal College of Psychiatrists, Occasional Paper Series.

Jones, D.P.H. (1996). Management of the sexually abused child. *Advances in Psychiatric Treatment,* **2**: 39–45.

Jones, D.P.H. (1997). Treatment of the child and the family where child abuse or neglect has occurred. In Helfer, R., Kempe, R., Krugman, R. (Eds.) *The Battered Child,* 5th edition, pp521–542. Chicago: University of Chicago Press.

Jones, D.P.H., Alexander, H. (1987). Treating the abusive family within the family care system. In Helfer, R., Kempe, R.S. (Eds.) *The Battered Child,* 4th edition. London: University of Chicago Press.

Kaufman, J., Zigler, E. (1989). The Intergenerational Transmission of Child Abuse. In Cicchetti, D., Carlson, V. (Eds.) *Child Maltreatment; Theory and Research on the causes and Consequence of Child Abuse and Neglect.* Cambridge: Cambridge University Press.

Kempe, R.S., Kempe, C.H. (1978). The untreatable family. In *Child Abuse.* London: Open Books, pp128–131.

Kitchur, M., Bell, R. (1989). Group psychotherapy with pre-adolescent sex abuse victims, literature review and a description of an inner city group. *International Journal of Group Psychotherapy,* **39**: 285–310.

Kroth, J.A. (1979). Family therapy impact on intrafamilial child sexual abuse. *Child Abuse and Neglect,* **3**: 297–302.

Levy, H., Markovic, J., Chaudhry, U., Ahart, S., Torres, H. (1995). Reabuse Rates in a Sample of Children followed for five years after discharge from a Child Abuse Inpatient Assessment Programme. *Child Abuse & Neglect,* **19**: 1363–1377.

Lutzker, J.R., Rice J.M. (1984). Project Twelve Ways, measuring outcome of a large in-home service for treatment and prevention of child abuse and neglect. *Child Abuse & Neglect,* **8**: 519–524.

Lynch, M.A., Roberts, J. (1982). *Consequences of Child Abuse.* London: Academic Press.

McBogg, P., McQuiston, M., Alexander, H. (1979). Circle House residential treatment programme. *Child Abuse & Neglect,* **3**: 863–867.

Nicol, A.R., Smith, J., Kay, B., Hall, D., Barlow. J., Williams, B. (1988). A focused casework approach to the treatment of child abuse: a controlled comparison. *J Child Psychol Psychiatry,* **29**: 703–711.

Oates, K..R., Bross, D.C. (1995). What have we learned about Treating Child Physical Abuse? A Literature Review of the Last Decade. *Child Abuse & Neglect,* **19**: 463–474.

Runtz, M., Schallow, J. (1997). Social support and coping strategies as mediators of adult adjustment following childhood maltreatment. *Child Abuse & Neglect,* **21**: 211–226.

Rutter, M. (1989). Intergenerational continuities and discontinuities in serious parenting difficulties. In Cicchetti, D., Carlson, V. (Eds.) *Child Maltreatment, Theory and Research on the Cause and Consequences of Child Abuse and Neglect.* Cambridge: Cambridge University Press.

Schetky, D.H., Angell, R., Morrison, C.V., Sack, W.H. (1979). A study of 51 cases of termination of parental rights. *Journal of the American Academy of Child Psychiatry*, **18**: 366–383.

Sharland, E., Seal, H., Crouche,r M., Aldgate, J., Jones, D.P.H. (1996). *Professional intervention in child sexual abuse.* London: Her Majesty's Stationery Office.

Smith, J.E., Rachman, S.J.(1984). Non-accidental injury to children: II. A controlled evaluation of a behavioural management programme. *Behaviour Research and Therapy*, **22**: 349–366.

Smith, J.E., Rachman, S.J., Yule, B. (1984). Non-accidental injury to children: III. Methodological problems of evaluative treatment research. *Behaviour Research and Therapy*, **22**: 367–383.

Spaccarelli, S., Kim, S. (1995). Resilience criteria and factors associated with resilience in sexually abused girls. *Child Abuse & Neglect*, **19**: 1171–82.

Taw, T.E. (1979). The issue of reinjury: An agency experience. *Child Abuse & Neglect*, **3**: 591–600.

Wald, M.S. (1982). State intervention on behalf of endangered children. *Child Abuse & Neglect*, **9**: 3–45.

Widom, K. (1988). Sampling biases and implications for child abuse research. *American Journal of Orthopsychiatry*, **58**: 260–270.

Wolfe, D.A., Bourdeau, P.A. (1987). Current issues in the assessment of abusive and neglectful parent-child relationships. *Behav Assess*, **9**: 271–290.

Wolfe, D.A., Aragona, J., Kaufman, K., Sandler, J. (1980). The importance of adjudication in the treatment of child abusers: Some preliminary findings. *Child Abuse & Neglect*, **4**: 127–135.

CHAPTER FIVE:

Partnership, collaboration and change under the Children Act

Tony Morrison

In 1989, Sir William Utting, then Chief Social Services Inspector, declared that the implementation of the Children Act 1989 would require a sea change of attitude across the board in re-orientating child welfare and child protection services to fulfil the Act's intentions. He suggested that such profound changes might well take a decade to occur. Five years after the Act actually came into force in England and Wales, Northern Ireland implemented virtually identical legislation from 4th November, 1996. As a trainer who regularly visits the region, watching fellow professionals in Northern Ireland prepare for this has revived many memories of the conflicting hopes, fears, confusions and anxieties, experienced in England and Wales in the run up to implementation.

What resonated most strongly has been the anxiety and temporary loss of confidence amongst even the most experienced child welfare professionals, across the agencies, about two things:

- whether with the new emphasis on partnership with parents, children would go unprotected;

- whether there would be the resources to fulfil the preventative ethos that underpins the Act.

This chapter explores a number of themes related to the key question as to what extent 'partnership' practice creates both necessary and sufficient conditions for therapeutic change in families in which significant harm has occurred. In exploring this a number of related questions are raised about both context and understandings of practice. These include:

- What organisational changes have occurred since the Act?

- How do these affect partnership and collaboration between agencies in child protection work?

- How does the above affect the prospects for therapeutic change in families in which abuse has occurred?

- To what extent is there now a shared understanding across agencies of 'partnership'?

- How might a general model of change (*Protchaska and DiClimenti, 1983*) enhance the prospects for effective partnership practice?

- How can a model of motivation assist professionals in making decisions as to which family situations can/cannot be managed on a non-statutory basis?

- What specific considerations apply in working with involuntary clients?

- What implications might this have for the management of services and training of staff?

These themes seek to integrate organisational and therapeutic perspectives on change. Thus the discussion is equally relevant to managers and practitioners, across the range of agencies involved with child protection work. The material will also extend the discussion in Chapter 2 on Howe's framework for participation. Clearly the scope of this chapter is potentially very wide, and therefore some aspects are dealt with more briefly, in particular discussion of the first three aspects listed above.

What organisational changes have occurred since the Act?

The past seven years have seen an escalation in both the extent and rate of organisational change across the public sector. No agency or discipline has been left unaffected. Managers are in many cases left breathless and often at least temporarily disorientated, in the face of such relentless demands on their physical, professional and emotional capacities to keep up with changes themselves and then to manage their staff through them. Reforming legislation has occurred in social services, health, education and criminal justice sectors, in pursuit of greater efficiency and effectiveness with the introduction of market principles against a backcloth of fiscal retrenchment. The resulting rationalisation of resources and priorities, decentralisation, fragmentation of central command structures, particularly in education, and health, have placed increasing strains on the fundamental ethos of multi-agency collaboration as a basis for child protection work.

How do these changes affect partnership and collaboration between agencies in child protection work?

Hallett (1995) has observed that inter-agency collaboration is at its best at the point of crisis (referral, investigation and initial case management), and much weaker both prior to the emergence of a crisis (prevention), and after the initial crisis has passed (therapeutic services). Yet as Gibbons (1995) points out, inter-agency collaboration is required just as much at the preventative and post-abuse stages, but health and education largely control both the universal and the specialist resources which promote child development and recovery from trauma.

Most professionals remain highly committed to the principle of multi-agency work as the basis for effective child protection. However these changes have reduced the time and resources available for working together, as individual agencies redefine their core business. Thus activity targets for health visitors, established to meet the health purchaser's specification may not allow for the previous level of an individual health visitor's involvement in inter-agency child protection work. Further, the expectation that all services should be costed, in order to measure value for money, has meant that collaboration is increasingly based on fiscal as opposed to inter-professional arrangements. Whilst multi-agency planning and commissioning of childrens' services is the way forward, (*Jones and Bilton, 1994*) as yet this is embryonic in nature. The result is that collaboration is currently dangerously over-dependent on the commitment and skills of individuals, rather than organisations, and thus too easily disrupted by their departure. Unfortunately this means that whilst the quality of response may be very good if it involves individuals committed to collaboration, it cannot guarantee or maintain that response across populations or over time. Effective child protection depends on *inter-organisational* not just *multi-disciplinary* working.

At the same time the numbers of child protection registrations having dropped significantly in 1992-3 after 'grave concern' was removed as a category, rose steadily until 1995 before levelling out in 1996–7.

Table 1

Total Registrations: England, Wales and Northern Ireland

1992	1993	1994	1995	1996	1997
42,174	35,633	37,986	38,146	35,551	N/K

Total Registrations: England only

38,600	32,500	34,900	34,954	32,351	32,369

Children added to the Register pa: England only

24,500	24,700	28,500	30,444	28,270	29,169

(DOH, 1995a and 1997)

Hallett and Birchall (*1992*) summarise these pressures when they write: "the atmosphere of chronic overstrain, unrealistic expectations on staff, desperately inadequate resources to cope with rapidly increased reportage of cases, and a limited fund of skills and knowledge confronting rising expectations that abuse should always be successfully managed."

Into this melting pot has more recently been added the debate arising from the publication of Child Protection: Messages from Research (*DOH, 1995b*) concerning the balance to be achieved between family support and child protection approaches. These findings, from some twenty post-Cleveland research projects have kindled a long standing debate about the pros and cons of an investigation-orientated child protection system in which resources are focused more on identification and risk assessment than on prevention, or post-abuse therapeutic services. Thus Gibbons (*1995*) found that "three quarters of the children and families drawn into the child protection system received no protective intervention" (*p151*). As for those who did receive a protective service, the majority of "registered children and their families received monitoring and limited practical help, rather than specific services aimed at compensating for the effects of maltreatment" (*p148*).

Thus one of the questions was whether a proportion of these referrals could have been better dealt with under section 17 of the Act where inquiries could have been made about the needs of these families for support in relation to issues such as poor parental care, or parent-adolescent disputes, where there was no specific indication of significant harm. In the longer term it will be important to see how registration trends are affected by this debate, particularly in the context of the long awaited revision of *Working Together*, expected later in 1998. Certainly the figures for England at least do not demonstrate a dramatic reduction in registration rates two years on from the publication of the *Messages from Research* (*DOH, 1995b*).

The aspirations of the Children Act are therefore mediated by an organisational context which has at least in the short term become less predictable, less stable and more conflictual as the competition for resources becomes ever more acute. Whilst the emphasis on contractual, accountable and targeted services may in the longer term result in strategic inter-agency partnerships for the planning, commissioning and evaluating of child protection services, in the short term at least 'partnerships' across agencies are under severe strain.

How then does this impact on partnership practice at the ground level and on the prospects for the kinds of change to which Gibbons (*1995*) refers that "gets to grips with the forces which produced the maltreatment and compensate for their effects on the child" (*p153*).

Impact of organisational changes on prospects for therapeutic changes

To explore this further it will be helpful to return to Howe's (*1992*) framework and examine the relationship between partnership relations among and within agencies, and those between professionals and families. In Chapter 2 Howe's partnership matrix was described as it applied to family-professional relations. This framework demonstrates a range of different relations depending on the degree of participation and the status of the client e.g.: voluntary versus involuntary. It will have been seen how voluntary client status does not guarantee participation if the workers' approaches are paternalistic or based on creating dependency. Conversely it will be noted that even where the client is involuntary, participation is possible if a social justice 'fair play' approach is made. Of course, although around three quarters of child protection cases are managed without recourse to court sanctions, it would be naive to suggest that these can be considered as voluntary clients in any psychological meaning of the term. They co-operate, at least at the outset, for fear of a more severe sanction.

Using Howe's framework it is therefore possible to see that natural justice principles, and 'partnership' under the Act, do not depend on equality. They depend rather on fairness and openness. This point is also made in the Challenge of Partnership in Child Protection:

"The objective of any partnership ... must be the protection and welfare of the child; partnership should not be an end in itself. Workers should consider the possibility of a partnership with each family based on openness, mutual trust, joint decision making and willingness to listen to families and to capitalise on their strengths. However words such as equality, choice and power have limited meaning at certain points in the child protection process" (*DOH, 1995c, 11–12*).

Even more importantly Howe distinguishes between partnerships based on natural justice principles which are designed to ensure fair play (transparency of roles, responsibilities, powers, open communication, decision making) and therapeutic partnerships which are based in contrast on a *psychological* contract for change. The natural justice partnership can therefore be considered an absolutely essential but not sufficient condition for therapeutic change. Whilst material aid and monitoring can be delivered through natural justice partnerships, it is only by combining natural justice and psychological approaches to partnerships that the conditions in which inter-personal changes can occur can be created. And it is these deeper level changes to the nature of family relationships that are crucial in responding to the high criticism – low warmth group in which the worst outcomes for children occur.

It may well be that the Act's real contribution thus far has been to reduce the extent of adversarial child protection relations between workers and families by ensuring a much greater degree of 'fair play'. However the achievement of 'fair play' is not an end in itself. The challenge is to increase the prospects and resources for moving to the next stage – the therapeutic partnership. For it is only at this point that it will be possible to tackle the 'forces that produce maltreatment' (*Gibbons, 1995*).

Inter-agency collaboration will be essential to achieve this level of therapeutic partnership, because no single agency has the resources or skills to do this alone. Therefore partnership needs to be seen as an *organisational* as well as a practice concept. As it will be shown in a reformulation of Howe's model, this means that the achievement of partnership practice with families and children, is contingent on the quality of partnership relations both within and between agencies. Much of this in turn depends on the extent to which agencies have developed a shared understanding about 'partnership' under this Act.

The challenge of *Partnership in Child Protection* (*DOH, 1995c*) helpfully, and for the first time, recognises that understandings about partnership in child protection have, and will continue to evolve. Four levels of partnership are distinguished which may vary between family members, and over time. They are:

i.   Providing information;

ii. Involvement but predominantly passive e.g.: attending a conference;

iii. Participation on an active basis, contributing to information and decision making;

iv. Partnership based on openness, mutual trust, joint decision-making and willingness to listen to, and be influenced by, families and to capitalise on their strengths.

To what extent is there a shared understanding of 'partnership' across agencies?

Whilst in broad terms, the ethos of seeking to work with families, wherever possible without recourse to statutory intervention, is now well accepted, confusions do remain about the detailed workings of partnership practice with involuntary clients. It is still not unheard of for professionals, mainly outside Social Services, to equate partnership with equality. Moreover what professionals believe in terms of their value base, may become distorted in practice by pressure, anxiety, lack of confidence and role confusion. The impact of anxiety on professional practice cannot be under-estimated (*Morrison, 1996*). Thus well intentioned professionals, with a commitment to a natural justice approach may begin to act adversarily or paternalistically in the kinds of organisational and inter-organisational conditions which are described below.

In addition there are much greater tensions over the organisational implications of the 'partnership' ethos for inter-agency collaboration. Using a modified version of Howe's model, differing perceptions of collaboration can be examined. In this version, voluntary and partici-patory relations between organisations are described as developmental, a more appropriate term then therapeutic. Looking at the four positions in Figure 1 – paternalism, strategic, play fair, and developmental – a number of key questions can be explored about the impact of each on the prognosis for achieving change in working with families where abuse has occurred.

The questions to be posed are:

i.   what attitudes to collaboration might each position hold?

ii.   what beliefs about change might each position hold?

iii. how might this affect partnership practice with families?

iv.   what implication might each position have for anti-discriminatory practice?

The descriptions of the attitudes and practice approaches generated by the different positions can be taken to represent potentially both inter and intra-organisational as well as individual professional responses. Rarely does one position encompass the complexity of an agency's approach, so that the responses may more realistically be seen to express different and conflicting positions held by different parts or sub-cultures *within* an organisation as well as differences *between* organisations.

ORGANISATIONAL PARTNERSHIP MODEL

	INVOLUNTARY	VOLUNTARY
NO PARTICIPATION	**STRATEGIC** Us v. the world Adversarial approach	**PATERNALISM** You need us Medical model approach
PARTICIPATION	**PLAY FAIR** Involving others Social justice approach	**DEVELOPMENTAL** Working and learning together Psychological approach

Howe (1992) as modified by Morrison (1996)   *Figure 1*

Paternalism

Here collaboration is viewed as an activity which is engaged in, as and when the agency deems fit, and only on its own terms. It involves others when it chooses. The agency views collaboration not as an obligation, but as a benefit it confers on other agencies/professionals. It is not therefore expected that the 'recipient' of this generosity should be anything other than grateful for the time and sharing of information, and should certainly not think to challenge what is offered/not offered, or how and when this occurs. The donor agency sees itself as having unique expertise, and finds it hard to respect others as having different but equally valid skills. It would not see itself as needing other agencies, as this is a one-way transaction.

Attitudes to change reflect this orientation. The professional is the expert. Clients are rarely involved in the formulation of the problem, nor in planning and implementing solutions. Instead their role is to accept what is offered with gratitude. Thus client involvement is minimal, and their presence in meetings is to answer questions and be 'given' the prescribed solution.

The assumed expertise, combined with the passive role expected of the client and the lack of attention to the client's definitions of their experience, means that the maintenance of inequality is an essential ingredient to this process. Furthermore it is assumed that this power will be used benignly for the good of the client as defined by the agency. Opportunities to challenge this are minimal, and failures are likely to be attributed either to the client or to other agencies. It is an oppressive environment, lacking in empathy, affecting not only external relations with clients and other agencies, but also contaminating internal staff and supervisory relations.

Strategic/Adversarial

Here collaboration is approached with considerable wariness and caution. Perceptions exist that collaboration will involve more losses than gains, that other agencies will exploit the process in order to gain territory or acquire resources at the expense of one's own agency. From this a siege mentality can emerge, characterised by 'watch your back', 'us versus the world', and 'win-lose' mentalities, in which boundaries are continuously defended, and little trust develops. Ulterior motives are constantly suspected. Territorial behaviours dominate interaction.

The result is that collaboration is frequently conflictual, and endless time is spent on negotiating the terms of engagement. Interaction between agencies is mediated through bureaucratic modes, such as memos, with an absence of informal or personal communication. Much written communication is taken up with complaining, disputing and dumping on other agencies. Internally in such agency contexts, the same behaviour may well be in evidence between parts of the organisation.

All of this distracts from a focus on the client, sometimes with potentially dangerous consequences. Indeed the agencies are so preoccupied with their own survival that clients may unwittingly become marginal to the agency's concerns. In such contexts client involvement in decision making is unpredictable, and there is little transparency of process. Change is perceived in conflict-model terms, resulting in a behaviourist contingency management outlook: "If the client won't do x, then we will withdraw our service ... or ... ". In extreme situations clients may even be seen as part of the enemy. Potentially the client's good relationship with another agency may be seen as a threat to one's own agency. Consequently there is a danger of collusive relationships with clients, evolving as part of the territorialism between agencies.

The lack of openness and trust, the high degree of mutual suspicion, and the power struggles being played out, make this too a potentially oppressive environment, not least because agency rather than client needs predominate. Thus the needs of minority groups, or those unable to vocalise their needs or dissatisfactions, are likely to be easily lost, resulting in passive levels of involvement only. The agency may have little interest in hearing about the client's experience or the impact of their intervention on the client.

Play fair

Here there is a basic belief that clients both need and have an entitlement to an effective multi-disciplinary service. Agencies are therefore concerned to ensure that all are clear about their roles and responsibilities. There is a focus on clarity of mutual expectations, processes of working together and about how clients will be involved in this. There is an emphasis on specificity and clear contracts in relations both with agencies and clients. An appreciation and respect exists for the different roles played by agencies/disciplines. This is manifested through careful thought about procedures, and commitment to multi-agency training. In contrast to the previous positions, here there is concern for the client's experience of agencies' interventions, and for the views and needs of staff who have to operate the child protection process.

In 'play fair', the prospects for change are perceived to be stronger, the greater the client's involvement in the process. Through this the client will be able to mobilise their own and their family's helping resources and strengths. Moreover there is a high level of awareness of the unintentional ways in which the intervention process can inhibit the client's strengths and demotivate the client from contemplating change. Thus practice is concerned to ensure that the client's perceptions and views are centre-stage, and that interventions at least do not do harm. Clients are seen as partners in the process.

This is an implicitly anti-oppressive approach, because it is client centred. Thus it is seen as important for instance to ensure in case conferences that the views of all participants are heard, regardless of occupational role, gender, ethnicity etc., on the basis of what they contribute to the debate. Thus the views of nursery nurses, foster carers, and black staff are actively sought. More widely, there is attentiveness to the needs of all staff, to ensure equality of access for instance to training and to anti-discriminatory ways of managing staff.

However difficulties can arise where there are conflicts of interest between parents/carers and children. This often reflects confusion between notions of fair play and equality, potentially leading to situations in which the concern with fair processes may obscure a focus on outcomes, and the need to use authority when children are in clear danger. Thus the level of partnership will need to be moderated to reflect the degree of protective action required, rather than vice versa. For instance agencies may restrict what information is given to a Schedule 1 offender if it is judged that to share more information will place a child or perhaps a female partner at risk. It is a reminder that partnership is a means to an end, the promotion of the welfare of the child, not an end in itself.

Developmental

Whilst this position shares almost all the positive elements of fair play just described, and is concerned with open and just processes, its vision is broader. Collaboration is seen as providing a dynamic model of positive and developmental processes which are intended to motivate both staff and clients to work for change. Although the emphasis on inter-agency role clarity and openness remains, there is an underlying commitment to an organic and developmental understanding of inter-agency work.

Working and learning together, equally from failures as successes, sharing risk, and pooling resources, characterise such an approach. This high degree of mutuality may more readily work at a multi-disciplinary team level rather than in relations between organisational entities, although aspects of this high level collaboration will occur inter-organisationally. Where this happens, there will also be an informal network of strong professional and inter-personal relationships at a managerial level which are the basis for the risk taking involved and the surrender of some organisational autonomy. It is also likely to be supported by active local multi-disciplinary networks, who interact not just at formal meetings such as case conferences, but at regular points outside the case management process (*McFarlane and Morrison, 1994*).

An important feature of this more dynamic approach is a focus on outcomes as well as process. Thus auditing of needs and evaluation of intervention impact are undertaken, not just at the level of outputs, e.g. what service was provided, but more importantly, what difference did it make for children and their families. The primary focus is thus on development and change, rather than on systems and process. Concern that children should be protected is seen as part of a wider commitment to enhance childrens' development and life chances.

In line with this developmental perspective, change is understood as most likely in conditions where not only the client is involved, but in which therapeutic relationships and resources are established and maintained over time. This approach seeks to integrate specific therapeutic input with the establishment of a pro-therapeutic environment, involving schools, carers and self help or volunteer groups who interact regularly with the family. The layers of damage, distortion, hurt and isolation that underlie the high criticism-low warmth families, are recognised. Care is taken to monitor outcomes for children, accepting that some children cannot return to their families. Again this is an anti-oppressive approach, because of its concern for the client, and the need to ensure that services are culturally appropriate in meeting both inter-personal and environmental needs.

It should be clear from these descriptions why collaboration between and within agencies is so linked to the quality and outcomes of partnership work with children and families. Rather like the child whose world is mediated through the quality of relationships between the parents, so the experience of vulnerable families in the child protection process is mediated through the modelling of multi-disciplinary relationships and behaviour. One cannot feel safe as an airline passenger whilst witnessing the crew arguing amongst themselves, or worse providing conflicting accounts of what is happening and what to do when the plane is in trouble.

Deficits in collaboration undermine the experience of partnership for families and reduce or even block the prospects for change. Positive outcomes cannot be sustained by even the most skilful practitioners, if the inter-agency context is anti-therapeutic. Individual successes will constantly be buried under the pile of collaborative failures. The foregoing discussion has sought to indicate which types of collaborative processes are likely to enhance or inhibit the prospects of positive outcomes for children.

The attitude of front line staff to the partnership ethos is powerfully affected by agency cultures. Many staff lack a basic sense of trust and confidence in their own agency, without which their ability to work empathically and skilfully with dysfunctional family dynamics is very impaired. Thus the front line of partnership, where workers seek to engage with families, can become an interaction between two parties neither of whom feel understood, valued, respected, prepared or supported (*Morrison, 1996*). Under such circumstances the likelihood of retreats into adversarialism, paternalism or collusion is all the more. As Calder (*1995*) notes "Partnership is loaded with possibilities, but it cannot offer a quick solution to entrenched problems". The same can also be said of inter-agency collaboration.

Prospects for therapeutic change

Plainly there are no easy formulae to eliminate the unintended and adverse effects on those families who need to be managed within the child protection process. Nor are there simple strategies to dramatically raise the number of positive outcomes from intervention. However what may be helpful is to focus thinking on basic questions. For it is through the development of shared meaning that we are most likely to improve the prospects that collaboration and partnership will indeed bring about change. These questions are therefore about the nature of change, rather than the machinery of the child protection system.

- what outcomes do we want from a child protection system?

- what broad understandings of motivation and change can guide collaborative effort?

- what considerations apply in working with involuntary clients?

What basic outcomes are required from a child protection system?

In relation to the overall goals of a child protection system three points can be made. First it should strive to keep out of the system those families who do not need to be in it, by ensuring that child protection is not the sole gateway to resources or collaboration. Secondly, it is important that there is a robust protective system for those children who require it. Thirdly, children and families who come into the child protection system should be guaranteed a comprehensive assessment of their needs, and an entitlement to a therapeutic service.

What model of motivation and change can guide collaborative effort?

If collaborative efforts are to achieve therapeutic outcomes, this can only happen where the inputs of different agencies are sufficiently congruent to ensure that different intervention methods and strategies do not become mutually contradictory. This requires the development of some inter-agency consensus about frameworks for understanding motivation and change. For instance if professional A considers that supportive approaches alone motivate people to change, whilst professional B considers that constructive use of discomfort may also be motivational, it can be seen how easily these two approaches may start to conflict and confuse.

Thus the development of some shared frameworks for understanding change, particularly in involuntary situations, would seem to be an essential step for agencies in creating collaborative partnerships for therapeutic change. This is not the same as prescribing particular methods of intervention, as different agencies offer intervention with different aspects of family life. But a general framework for change and motivation would potentially offer some common language in which to assess motivation and plan for change. Too often, rush and pressure precludes such discussion, which proceeds along the assumption of commonality until it suddenly becomes uncomfortably clear that different premises about change had been in existence all along.

In the previous edition, Protchaska and DiClementi's *Comprehensive Model of Change* (1982) was presented (*see Figure 2*). Since then, experience with professionals from all disciplines has confirmed that, although this is not the only general model of change, it provides a valuable general framework to begin a detailed discussion about change. Secondly, because this model is about the overall process of change, it does not prescribe specific methods of change. The model allows for different therapeutic interventions, from different agencies at different stages. Finally many professionals have commented how relevant this model is to circumstances other than child protection work, in terms of their own experiences of change. This is a factor which might reduce the dangers of unintentionally asking clients to make changes at a pace, and in a manner, which bears little resemblance to one's own life experiences. The model which has itself been updated by the authors, is now re-presented but with additional material from this author on assessing and enhancing motivation.

The model is discussed in the context of child protection issues, where there may be a need for external sanctions via court orders, and where in general terms the client's engagement in the system is involuntary at the outset at least. However the model would also apply to family support work where the context is likely to be more truly voluntary.

The model's basic premises are that change is a matter of balance, and that people change their behaviour when there are more motivational forces in favour of change than in favour of status quo. Thus motivating people to change involves positively weighting, increasing or establishing

COMPREHENSIVE MODEL OF CHANGE

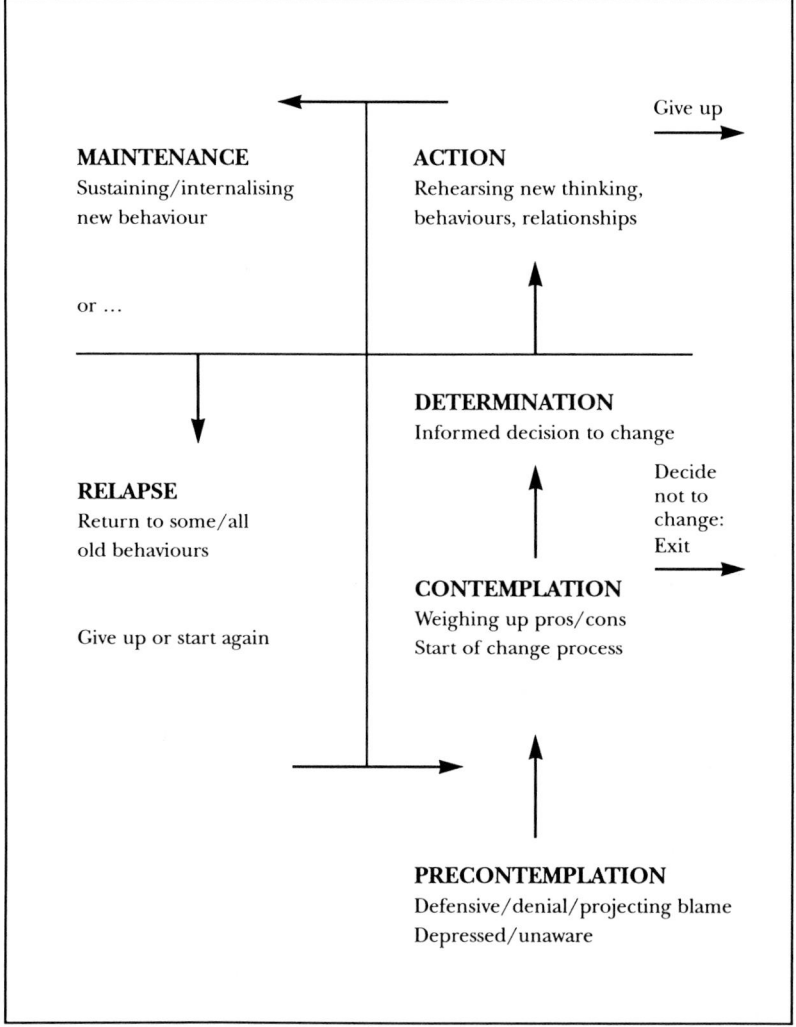

MAINTENANCE
Sustaining/internalising
new behaviour

or ...

ACTION
Rehearsing new thinking,
behaviours, relationships

Give up

DETERMINATION
Informed decision to change

RELAPSE
Return to some/all
old behaviours

Give up or start again

Decide
not to
change:
Exit

CONTEMPLATION
Weighing up pros/cons
Start of change process

PRECONTEMPLATION
Defensive/denial/projecting blame
Depressed/unaware

DiClementi, 1991

Figure 2

motivators for change, whilst actively removing, decreasing or re-framing barriers to change, whether material, or psychological, individual or environmental. Because change is seen as a matter of balance, ambivalence is a continuing feature of the change process, acting like a tide that ebbs and flows, sometimes generating small currents that temporarily distract the course of change, but at other times, creating deep turbulence throwing the course of change into a whirlpool of indecision, prompting rapid retreat to safer, calmer and better known waters.

Motivation is also seen to reside not in individuals (*Miller, 1991*) but in an interactional context, in which professionals are highly significant figures, especially where the future security of the family is in question. However family, friends, community support and expectations all form the wider motivational network, containing both pro and anti-therapeutic elements. This is part of the argument for making use of family group conferences where this wider network can be brought into focus and utilised. For Miller (*1991*) whose work on motivational interviewing is built around this model of change, a principle task for workers is the motivation of the client.*

Pre-Contemplation

The vast majority of families are at this point where agencies are beginning to make enquiries following a report of suspected abuse. They are scared and anxious at the arrival of child protection professionals, and therefore often defensive, angry and reluctant to look at difficulties within. They were fine before 'we' arrived. In contrast to this more common presentation, may be a helpless, passive response, in which parents seem unable to comprehend what has happened to their child, and appear not to react to the very serious things that professionals are saying to them. This response may result from shock, depression or other more profound mental disorders. Their pre-contemplation may therefore be less conscious.

At this stage the agencies' combined anxieties may drive them on prematurely into the Action stage, wanting to get something done. In reality many parents are probably still at pre-contemplation at the end of the first case conference, and ready to agree to any child protection plan out of fear for what may happen if they do not. But as the model

---

* Although only limited reference can be made to Miller's work here, his book provides one of the most practical, ethical and research based approaches to interviewing.

suggests it is essential that workers understand what stage the client is at, otherwise interventions and plans will be incongruent with the client's stage of change, and are more likely to fail. No change is possible whilst the client is in pre-contemplation. Change can only begin once the client is enabled to move into the Contemplation stage.

Contemplation

Here the client begins to consider the possibility that there is a problem, and explore whether they feel able to tackle it and make progress. Part of their very early motivation may come from the imposed intervention of the agency system, perhaps via registration of their child, or the threat of court action, giving a potent message that things must change. This in itself is not anti-therapeutic but much will depend on whether this external motivation can be transformed into internal motivation. The ability of workers to combine the use of external sanctions with the engagement of families is crucial if it is to lead to change. Early allocation of workers and pro-vision of supportive services are important in facilitating this process.

It is here that careful assessment and enhancement of motivation becomes pivotal, not only for the professional system, but equally for the family. For it is the family, who must be assisted in looking painfully at them-selves, coming to terms with what they see, counting the real costs of what change will mean, and identifying benefits and goals that have real meaning for them. This is the work of Contemplation.

It is too easy to assume, either that clients must be motivated before they walk into the room if change is to happen, or conversely, to accept a vague promise that they will do whatever we ask, as evidence of motivation. It is imperative to distinguish between ambivalence, com-pliance, and change. Some children have suffered from our failure to distinguish between compliance and change.

7 Steps of Contemplation

In an attempt to assist workers at this crucial stage of Contemplation, this author developed a 7 Step mini-model of Contemplation. Its intention is in guiding workers both in assessing client motivation, and planning interviews and other strategies aimed at increasing motivation. The 7 Steps focus on moving from Pre-Contemplation to Determination, between the first dawning recognition of a problem through to the development of a detailed understanding of, and commitment to, what change will involve. The 7 Steps can also be used by supervising managers or case conference chairs to elicit concrete evidence about the client's readiness to change as a basis for planning and case management. It has also been used directly with clients.

The 7 Steps of Contemplation

1) I accept there is a problem:

e.g.: "I accept my child has a fractured skull". At this first step of Contemplation there may only be minimal agreement that there is a problem, but this needs to be capitalised on, and not rejected. Clearly if further progress is not made, this will not be a sufficient level of motivation for change to occur, and may indicate the need for external protective controls in the form of court orders.

2) I accept I have some responsibility for the problem:

e.g.: "I lost my temper that day because she wouldn't take her bottle". At this stage it is not necessary, or even realistic, for total responsibility to be taken by the client for their actions, but there has to be some recognition of personal influence in the identified problems. It is the task of further work to develop a wider understanding of difficulties, context and contributory factors.

Note: it is essential to distinguish between admission and responsibility. A person can admit without accepting responsibility, and therefore admission is not necessarily evidence of motivation, nor of reduced risk e.g.: "I hit him, and he'll get the same again if he doesn't learn".

3) I have some discomfort about the problem

e.g.: "I don't like what has happened, it was wrong". Without some degree of internal dissonance, the motivation will remain external, and may be no more than disguised compliance, covering an underlying resentment at having to cooperate with the agencies. Internal discomfort reveals that the client's behaviour is at some level at odds with their values and beliefs about what is appropriate.

4) I believe that things must change

e.g.: "We can't go on having these rows in front of the children." Here there is the realisation that something must change, but this does not mean that the client knows what this is, or how to replace unhelpful behaviours with more appropriate responses. It is also at this stage that the client may say in desperation: "I'll do whatever you say". Whilst there is now significant motivation, the client has two further steps to take if they are to make a confident attempt at change.

5) I can see that I can be part of the solution

e.g.: "I have some strengths, support and self confidence to know that I am capable of making some changes, however small." Eliciting the client's sense of self efficacy is perhaps the most frequently over-looked part of motivational work, despite the fact that Bandura's work (*1977*) found that self efficacy was the most effective predictor of change e.g.: that I see myself as being competent to make changes. Miller (*1991*) sees the aim of motivational interviewing as helping the client to make their own arguments for change, and exploring their ambivalence about change. Too often workers unintentionally take this process out of clients' hands, by suggesting, persuading, sometimes cajoling them with arguments that have meaning for professionals but not necessarily for clients. Ambivalence needs to be seen more as an alliance than a barrier to change.

6) I can make a choice

e.g.: "Even though I did not want my child on the Register, I recognise that I still have choices about how I respond to what is happening, and can play a part in what will happen next." The recognition of a choice point(s) is important in clarifying within the client's mind that they have some power to choose, even if the choices are small or limited in scope. This is particularly important in working with involuntary situations (*Ivanoff, Blythe and Tripodi, 1994*). Later in the process it also helps them if difficulties arise to recognise a clear decision point, particularly if they come under pressure from parts of their family to give up or withdraw co-operation with agencies.

7) I can see the next steps toward change

e.g.: "I know something practical I am going to do next week to start this process. " At this point delay in services, or allocation of new workers can be fatal. The client is ready to make an informed choice for change (Determination) but delay, whilst they are acutely conscious of all their problems, may well prove overwhelming, resulting in retraction and retreat into the earlier stages.

Determination:

This is closely allied to the sixth and seventh steps of Contemplation, as the client makes a more formal expression of: the changes they wish/ need to make; what specific goals are to be achieved; how the client and workers will cooperate in moving towards these; and what rewards and changes will occur once these goals are met – for instance deregistration; or the removal of court orders. It may well be that a series of mini contracts for change are needed as progress will be incremental and achieved in small stages. Again it is important to emphasise the danger of making these contracts prematurely when the client is barely out of pre-contemplation.

Action

Research into treatment has shown the importance of targeting specific interventions for specific problems, in an ordered sequence where there are multiple problems. Action could include both direct intervention work – behavioural work, parent-skill classes, as well as material aid and other supportive services designed to alleviate stress and poverty. It might include individual or family work to improve relationships and attachment. Thus it can be seen how this general model of change can accommodate a range of different interventions as long as the intervention is matched to where the client is up to.

Maintenance

By this stage the emphasis moves to consolidating changes already made. This may be achieved through rehearsal and testing of newly acquired skills and coping strategies over time and under different conditions. More specific attention also needs to be paid to relapse prevention work, aimed at anticipating stresses and triggers that may undermine newly acquired coping skills. Without this even apparently minor stresses can cause a sudden loss of confidence, placing the client in high risk situations in which the unwanted previous patterns that are harmful to children may return. This is not the same as predicting failure, but rather recognises that unforeseen stresses are likely to occur. These need to be anticipated, and strategies and local support generated to cope with, or exit quickly from such scenarios. Given their histories, for many young parents the boundary between being in control and out of control is very fine, so that small and unexpected stresses can easily threaten their sense of being in control.

This aspect of treatment work is sometimes given little or no space, as the pressure for resources requires rapid turnover. Typically a family may make significant progress in a family centre, as a result of which the child is deregistered, and services are terminated. However if changes have not been sufficiently integrated to daily life, and are still dependent on the supportive presence of family centre staff, new stresses may quickly overwhelm their fledgling confidence and skills, causing relapse.

Relapse

One of the strengths of this cyclical model is that is allows for the reality that few people succeed first time round. Change comes from repeated efforts, re-evaluation, renewal of commitment and incremental successes. However the model distinguishes between *lapse* and *relapse*.

Lapses occur when individuals/families get themselves into high risk situations – for instance couples beginning to argue again over who should discipline the child. At this point it is vital that the couple recognise the danger, and put into action their relapse prevention plan – for instance to call a neighbour round while each have a cooling off period.

In contrast a relapse occurs with a return to the unwanted behaviour – in this case abuse of a child, which is clearly not desirable, and for which there may be serious consequences for the family's future. Lapse is thus part of, and not simply an enemy of change. In some cases where the risks associated with *relapse* to the child are high, court orders may be required to monitor this process and to ensure that contingency plans will protect children from further harm should the need arise. This illustrates some of the considerations that apply to this model where the context of work is an involuntary one.

Working with involuntary clients

In concluding discussion about this model of change a number of points about engaging involuntary clients should be made. First as Behroozi (*1992*) reminds us, the method of the client's entry into the system has considerable impact on the prognosis for constructive engagement with it. Being forced to engage in change is likely to increase the client's sense of failure, uncertainty and low self efficacy, which in turn generates defensiveness, resentment and degrees of non-compliance. It is important therefore that these feelings are explored at the outset.

Secondly as Ivanoff et al (*1994*) comment, workers' attitudes to these clients are very influential on their response. Ivanoff et al suggest that it is important to remember that although these clients' lives appear very different to those of professionals, there are in fact more similarities than differences: for instance sometimes professionals too are careless, chaotic or hurt other people.

Thirdly, the same authors comment that due to barriers created by the involuntary context, clients may not have the opportunity to build positive relations with workers. Workers should therefore keep in mind that lack of client co-operation may reflect the context as much as the worker's skills. This simple caveat might serve to reduce the chance of defensive manoeuvres on the part of workers when they experience silence, or hostility from such clients.

Fourthly care needs to be paid to preparing the client for their role as a client, and continuous attention is then required to ensure that the client is clear about the rules of engagement in terms of: role and powers of workers; expectations of the client; how the worker will respond to non-compliance; options and choices for the client; specific goals; opportunities for early success and incentives for progress (*Ivanoff et al, 1994*).

Fifthly and perhaps most fundamental, whilst making a constructive relationship is more difficult in these circumstances, it remains the key to everything else. As Ivanoff et al (*1994: 20*) state "although it is difficult to develop trust and rapport with clients who do not believe you want or know how to help them, we believe it is possible with almost all clients".

Conclusions

It is a good time to review progress of the Children Act. The challenges of taking the next steps in fulfilling the high aspirations set by this piece of legislation are both demanding and exciting. What might be some of the practical measures to consider in enriching and deepening the effectiveness of partnership practice?

1. ACPCs need to work more clearly on establishing a clear philosophy of intervention, and begin to specify outcomes;

2. Managers need training about broad therapeutic principles, so as to inform service development, procedures and care management and planning;

3. The critical role of reflective supervision must be reasserted in social work agencies, and other agencies need to develop reflective opportunities for their staff;

4. Multi-disciplinary training should contain some input on therapeutic principles and on the assessment and enhancement or motivations;

5. The purpose of the initial child protection case conference should primarily be to agree the need for and detail of plans to safeguard the child, and initial child protection plans should not necessarily be considered as therapeutic contracts for change;

6. Core groups should be seen as the principle multi-agency forum for therapeutic planning, and be given greater support and prominence for this role;

7. Family group conferences should be utilised more frequently as a motivational catalyst;

8. Assessment needs to focus as much on enhancing the client's level of motivation as on collecting information to share with other professionals;

9. There is a need for widespread investment in training front line child protection staff in motivational interviewing approaches. The vast majority of helping professionals, with the exception of police, have received little or no interviewing training;

10. There is a need to ensure that relapse prevention work is integrated into treatment services.

There are as will be evident from the above no simple ways of making a complex system respond better to a complex problem. No child protection system can easily reconcile and integrate safe-guarding and therapeutic activities, for both are and will continue to be required. However there are, as this chapter has suggested, ways at both strategic and practice levels in which the therapeutic potential of the child protection system can be enhanced.

Bibliography

Bandura, A. (1977). Self-efficacy: Towards a unifying theory of behavioural change. *Psychological Review,* **84(2)**: 191–215.

Behroozi, C. (1992). Groupwork with Involuntary Clients: Remotivating Strategies, *Groupwork,* **5(2)**: 31–41.

Calder, M. (1995). Child Protection: Partnership and Paternalism. *British Journal of Social Work,* **25(6)**.

DiClementi, C. (1991). Motivational Interviewing and the Stages of Change. In Miller, W., Rollnick, S., (Eds.) (1991) *Motivational Interviewing.* London: Guilford Press.

DOH (1995a). *Children and Young People on Child Protection Registers.* London: Government Statistical Service.

DOH. (1995b). *Child Protection: Messages from Research.* London: HMSO.

DOH. (1995c). *The Challenge of Partnership in Child Protection.* London: HMSO.

Gibbons, J., Conroy, S., Bell, C., (1995). *Operating the Child Protection System: A Study of Child Protection Practices in English Local Authorities.* University of East Anglia, HMSO: London.

Hallett, C., Birchall, E. (1992). *Co-ordination in Child Protection: A Review of the Literature.* HMSO, p303.

Hallett, C. (1995). *Inter-agency Co-ordination in Child Protection.* University of Stirling, HMSO: London.

Howe, D. (1992). Theories of helping, empowerment and participation. In Thoburn, J. (Ed.) *Participation in Practice – Involving families in child protection.* University of East Anglia, Norwich. p39 .

Jones, A., Bilton, K., (1994). *The Future Shape of Childrens Services.* London: National Childrens Bureau.

Ivanoff, A., Blythe, B., Tripodi, T., (1994). *Involuntary Clients in Social Work Practice.* New York: Aldine de Gruyter.

McFarlane, T., Morrison, T. (1994). Learning and Change: Outcomes of Inter-agency for Child Protection. *Child Care in Practice: Jo. of Multi-disciplinary Child Care Practice in Northern Ireland,* **1(2)**: 33–44.

Miller, W., Rollnick, S., (1991). *Motivational Interviewing.* London: Guilford Press.

Morrison, T. (1996). Partnership and Collaboration: Rhetoric and Reality, *Child Abuse and Neglect,* **20(2)**: 127–140.

Protchaska, J., DiClementi, C., (1982). Transtheoretical Therapy: Towards a more integrative model of change. *Psychotherapy: Theory, Research and Practice,* **19(3)**.

CHAPTER SIX:

Cultural and ethnic perspectives on significant harm: its assessment and treatment

Annie Lau

The Children Act places a requirement to work in partnership with the families of children towards whom a service is being proposed, whether this service is one of assessment of need, of significant harm, of treatability, or of provision of alternative accommodation. The 'partnership' requirement applies regardless of whether the arrangement is voluntary, as in a needs assessment, or involuntary, as would follow a Care Order. The concept of partnership implies that one so informs oneself that one can take the views of parents into account in making plans for the child. This is difficult enough in the adversarial context in which child care proceedings normally take place; it becomes doubly difficult when one is dealing with an ethnic minority family.

In this paper I shall attempt to address some relevant issues which may serve as practice guidelines. I am of Chinese ethnic origin and come from a traditional, hierarchical Singapore Chinese family. My early professional training was in Canada, and since 1979 I have worked in the United Kingdom as a Consultant in Child and Adolescent Psychiatry. The case examples used in this paper reflect my current practice.

When one is called out in an emergency to investigate an allegation of abuse, what does one need to think about? What is the worker's previous experience of working with ethnic minorities – is this 'coloured' by frustration and a sense of failure? How does one join or engage with these families, explore sources of strength and competence, look at the social and family context in which the alleged difficulties in individual or group functioning have given rise to professional concern?

Sources of strength, individual and family competence, are often to be found in the ethnocultural roots and traditions of the group. Religious belief, for example, often provides a source of important cognitive orienting concepts by which the individual or group structures value systems, role relationships and expectations within the family.

These belief systems and value orientations also provide a framework in which crises in life-cycle transitions can be successfully managed. Similarly, extended family traditions with 'old fashioned' concepts of family honour, filial piety (where loyalties to parents take precedence over all other loyalties), and 'reciprocal obligations' which ensure an enduring network of kinship loyalties have in many traditional, hierarchical families proved to be indispensable in ensuring family survival. However, conflict between traditional family values and those of more egalitarian, nuclear family structures may generate unbearable family tensions leading to family breakup, loss of morale and self-esteem, and abuse inflicted on more vulnerable members of the family.

In order to be able to assess abuse and the presence of significant harm in the different societal contexts found in the diverse racial and ethnic groups in the United Kingdom, one needs an appreciation of the range of this diversity, and the variations within ethnic groupings from traditional to modern/egalitarian. It is important to start out with an understanding of one's own ethnocultural roots and value systems. The worker from a family background with an egalitarian role model, and non-hierarchical relationships among the siblings as a valued norm, may find it difficult to work in a context where the father is the 'head of the household', as will be found in the majority of Asian and Vietnamese families in which special rights and responsibilities are conferred on older siblings, especially the eldest son. Similarly it would be difficult not to over-identify with the marginal adolescent who feels the only way she could protest against family expectations of an impending arranged marriage is by taking an overdose. It may be for the worker that the very idea of an arranged marriage is itself so odious that he/she forgets to explore other factors in family functioning where deficiencies may have led to the present crisis, for example, failure of mechanisms for conflict resolution and tension diffusion, or the presence of other serious problems like parental alcoholism or the existence of gambling debts.

The worker needs to be able to maintain a stance of professional neutrality, in order to facilitate and mobilise the family's capacity to make choices instead of making decisions for them. Normative assumptions about personhood in a family may interfere significantly with the need to be neutral. In order to mobilize strengths based on ethno-cultural roots, one needs to know what these strengths are before one can devise a strategy to mobilize them.

How then does one learn about these differences? Can and should one 'find out from the client'? In an emergency assessment situation one is under a great deal of pressure to make judgements. It is however important to realise we all make judgements on the basis of what we think intuitively is right. The difficulty comes about when these 'intuitive judgements' are based on ethnoculturally defined values. This is compounded when the worker's only experience of particular ethnic groups is in the grossly abnormal context of an assessment under the Children Act. One cannot then depend on these highly disadvantaged and stressed clients, who may or may not be behaving in a deviant manner, to teach you about cultural values in their own community. One needs previous experiences with normally functioning members of that ethnic community, where one can see the cultural assumptions and practices with which one disagrees, operating within the life of that community.

In the spirit of true partnership, it would be helpful for local authorities to discuss the question of significant harm and procedures for investigation and assessment with community representatives of the main ethnic minority groups in their areas. This may involve religious organisations or community associations and will enable valuable links to be established before crises occur. Aspects of communication, for example link workers, can then be addressed and community views ascertained, while misunderstandings can be clarified. Local authorities can then operate in a context in which they feel supported by elders from ethnic communities.

From a practical perspective I would suggest that the following findings would require immediate steps towards a thorough investigation, whether or not the worker was familiar with ethnocultural issues that may have a bearing on the case:

- the presence of actual physical injury;

- discrepancy between the child's account of events leading to the injury and the explanation offered by parents or caretakers;

- corroborative evidence from another agency with considerable opportunity to observe and report on the child's status, e.g. school nursery or day centre.

The following areas pose common dilemmas in the assessment of significant harm with regard to ethnic families:

- family structures that do not conform to Western European norms;

- 'culture bound' symptoms;

- culture-determined child-rearing practices.

Family structures that do not conform to Western European norms

1. Single parent Afro-Caribbean families

Despite the rise in single parent families in the UK, the white one-parent family is still widely regarded as deviant from the Western European ideal. In the same way, society still views the family structure of single-parent Afro-Caribbean families as deviant. Studies of working-class family structure in the West Indies, for example Henriques (*1949*) clearly show the stability of the matricentral family grouping, around a consanguineous basis rather than a conjugal basis. Extended family links are often built around mother's blood relationships and a strong sense of kinship extends beyond the immediate mother-child unit, in working class families. Long established links albeit 'informal', as for example godparents or grandfather's long standing co-habitee, may be invested with the same degree of authority and influence in family matters as the biological grandparent in a traditional Asian family. Thus for the single parent Black mother, her links with her mother and brothers are extremely important. In father's absence, maternal uncle was often the most important authority figure in a young Black boy's upbringing.

2. Extended family groupings in the same household

The assessment and management of intergenerational conflict in the same household is often a difficult one for therapists from a Western European nuclear family structure. One needs to know what authority structure exists, and what rules govern role relationships and expectations of behaviour; and how the presenting problem is linked to the rules and beliefs.

Case example: An infant was admitted to a paediatric ward with a second head injury in 6 months. The mother admitted responsibility for both accidents, and said on the first occasion the child had fallen out of her rocker while rocking vigorously, and on the second she had been careless and the pushchair had slipped down the stairs with the child still in it while she was busy unloading the shopping. Paediatric staff reported the mother to be warm and attentive towards the baby in hospital, and appropriately involved in her care. We felt, however, that something was not quite right.

I asked to see the family, from a traditional Sikh background. They were initially unwilling to disclose 'private' family matters until I pointed out that their family honour could be involved. It then emerged that the mother was in an extremely vulnerable situation. This was a family where she was the only daughter in law to have come from Kenya, whereas the others were all British born. Being less conversant with British ways, she had accepted the role of being the family childminder for all the pre-school children in the family while the other women went out to work. In the mornings therefore she had been overwhelmed with the pressures of providing childcare to four children including her own baby, and was also expected to do the shopping. Out of a sense of pride, and the need to prove her 'worth' to the family, she had not complained or asked for help from her sisters in law. A steep flight of stairs led directly to a narrow kitchen, and she had been putting the groceries away when her four year old nephew pushed the push-chair down the stairs. To complain about the behaviour of a senior sister-in-law's son would have been difficult, and challenged the hierarchy in the female network.

This family was helped to move from a position in which the young wife was being asked for a solution she could not give, to one in which the family could accept collective responsibility for protecting her and the children. The strategy was one of mobilizing family strengths though invoking the concept of family honour. Thus the therapist respected and accepted the authority structure of the family and its rules, one of the most important of which was the principle of inter-dependence.

Culture bound symptoms

Ethnic minority clients may present with maladaptive behaviour and symptoms influenced by the religious and symbolic language of the culture of origin. This may include a preoccupation with ghosts in incomplete mourning (*Henriques, 1951*); or spirit possession in conservative Muslim families or Chinese families from a rural background, often activated in a context of insoluble family conflict. Even though the symptoms and behavioural patterns may not fit established patterns of deviance in the wider British context, still the cultural patterning would be familiar to members of the same ethno-cultural group and may not be seen therefore as irrational and inexplicable. The symptoms and behavioural patterns may conform to cultural expectations of how one gains entry to the sick role. For example in Chinese communities depressed patients most commonly present with somatic complaints, and in the Chinese language depressed affects are couched with reference to the body.

Transient psychotic states in which the long term prognosis is usually good, are also found more commonly by psychiatrists in patients from an ethnic minority background. This needs to be taken on board in the assessment of future parenting capacity.

Case example: An Afro-Caribbean mother was felt by attending medical staff to have made a good recovery from a stress induced psychotic state.

She was still however anxious about her housing conditions and despite support from housing officers, had not been re-housed. While in a psychotic state her symptoms had a marked sexual content. Her social worker refused to support her request to have her children removed from the At Risk register on the grounds that she was still abnormally pre-occupied with sexual matters and the children were therefore still at risk.

As a consultant to the system I was told by the social worker that on recent home visits the mother would talk incessantly about 'cocks' and ask for help to get rid of them. She would also be abnormally concerned about the state of her children's bottoms. The social worker was white and said the relationship with the mother was not a comfortable one, and she was hard to understand.

I interviewed the mother on her own initially. There were no signs of mental illness. She had however a strong Afro-Caribbean accent. She said she had seen her social worker recently and on each occasion had tried hard to tell her there were cockroaches all over the place especially in the summer heat and could not understand why she did not take her seriously.

I also saw her with her children, aged 3 and 5. At one point they had to go to the toilet and I encouraged them to go by themselves. After they had left the room the mother said she usually had to make sure they cleaned their bottoms properly. On the children's return I inspected the bottoms. Neither child had wiped her bottom properly; the anuses were red and faecal matter was still present.

This was a case in which the social worker's professional neutrality had been compromised by communication and relationship difficulties with the client. It also included a lack of understanding of the nature of transient psychoses. The social worker had been accused of being racist, which made her even more defensive.

Culture determined child-rearing practices

Given the importance of inter-dependence and family connectedness across the generations as a goal for the socialisation of the young, it should not be surprising that patterns of child-rearing in traditional extended families would be different. The child from a traditional Asian or Vietnamese family may be sleeping with mother or grandmother for many years; indeed co-sleeping arrangements are often preferred in these families even though there may be adequate space for individual bedrooms. As the child grows up, he/she will have frequent and regular contact with members of the extended family. Through regular participation in family rituals such as meals, outings, festivals, religious events, the child learns his/her place in the kinship system and the rules governing relationships, and expected behaviour. Thus an older sibling will learn to take responsibility for a younger sibling; or to contribute to the family welfare by helping in the shop on the weekend. It will be a source of pride to "so behave that your parents will be proud of you". The young person learns the importance of maintaining the honour of the family by his or her public actions. Within the family boundary, he/she will also learn the importance of manoeuvres for diffusing tension in the family. Discipline is usually strict; the family cannot afford to lose face in the community. A fuller discussion of the differences in family developmental tasks in traditional extended families is to be found in *Psychological problems in adolescents from ethnic minorities* (*Lau, 1990*).

Refugee families

Families with a refugee background will need to be handled with particular understanding for the traumatic stresses which have been part of the family's recent experience. Adults will to a varying extent carry features of Post Traumatic Stress Disorder. For many, the stress of not being able to communicate in English will be extremely disabling, particularly for recent arrivals to this country.

Case example: Two boys aged 6 and 9 were referred to a Child Guidance Clinic by the school with concerns for their 'cruel and sadistic' behaviour, which included pushing other children down the stairs. They had arrived in the borough some two months previously, speaking no English. The family were political refugees from a Francophone African country. Both parents had been victims of torture and mother bore obvious scars on her arms. The clinic team met with the mother in her home with an interpreter. She said her husband was still in the country of origin and in prison. The boys did not know their father was missing and were told he was away on business. The mother described the boys as well-behaved at home and not a source of concern. We noted there were several letters offering health checks for the baby of about 6 months that had not been responded to. The mother spoke no English and did not know anyone who could translate or interpret for her.

Several follow-up sessions were then unattended without notice. On one occasion we arrived at the house to find the children had been left in the care of the oldest child aged 10, who did not know where mother was. The children seemed calm and settled, however, including the baby. On a subsequent home visit we found father, who had just arrived in the country after being smuggled out. He felt the need to be wary; there were likely to be death squads after him given his political status back home. He had clear symptoms of Post Traumatic Stress Disorder, with recurring nightmares and somatic symptoms. When informed about the school's concerns his first response was to be angry and he threatened the school with litigation. At the same time the school was frustrated with the lack of resources available to help them with the children's language needs.

These refugee parents were particularly vulnerable on account of their refugee status and past experiences of overwhelming trauma and loss. These experiences, and distrust of bureaucracy, affected their capacity to negotiate with the school. Father's unreasonably threatening attitude at the school obviously reflected the violence of his recent past, as well as the family's bewilderment at the uncertain present. Mother also could not understand our worry about the 'children being left alone'. The missed sessions had to do with necessary trips to the Home Office which she had to keep secret as the discussions were about her husband. The children were left in the care of the eldest child who she felt was adequate to the task. The children's behavioural disturbances were under-standable in terms of their confusion at not knowing what was happening to their father, and at the same time realising something was upsetting to mother but could not be talked about.

Placement issues

Given the massive over-representation of Afro-Caribbean and mixed race children in care, discussion on placement issues of ethnic minority children has largely focused on the special needs of this group. There is currently considerable debate on the same race versus transracial placement issue, relevant to adoption and fostering. Tizard had questioned whether even the concept of a 'positive racial identity' is a valid entity, as current research has failed to demonstrate links with self-esteem. The Children Act however clearly says race, language, religion and culture need to be taken on board in placement considerations.

Case example: The adoptive parents of a 10 year old boy of mixed race origins (White-Afro-Caribbean) complained of his 'attitude' problems. He would come home from school in a bad mood and get into an argument invariably with his father. Both adoptive parents were white, as was the other adopted child from infancy, a girl. Eventually on direct exploration he said it would be easier for him in his family if he were White, because he would not be called 'Nigger' by both his cousin and the boys in his school. He felt his parents did nothing about the racist abuse both within the family and outside it. The parents had told him it was 'just name calling' and he had to learn to put up with it and not get into fights. I noticed that I had to draw attention to the racist aspects of what the parents referred to as 'name-calling' as they were anxious to minimise the racial differences between them. In fact it became apparent that racial differences were not discussed. In time however it felt safe to do so and the parents appreciated their son's particular needs for support for his racial identity within the family as well as the school. This led to a considerable improvement in the relationship between the boy and his father.

Case example: An adolescent girl of mixed UK White-Hong Kong Chinese parentage was placed in care following allegations of abuse. The girl was classified as Black, assigned a black social worker and placed with a Black family. In this case, the social worker as well as the foster family turned out to be Afro-Caribbean. The girl's Chinese father found it difficult to think of his daughter living, as he put it, with 'Black devils'.

Issues of ethnicity and language had not been explored directly with the girl who had been exhibiting extremely disturbed behaviour, including wrist-cutting and repeated suicidal threats, as it was felt by professionals involved this may precipitate further disturbance.

As a consultant to the network, I was allowed to interview the girl after I reported my separate interviews with the parents elicited the information that she had been a fluent Chinese speaker. In fact the mother had been enraged by the conversation between this girl and her father in Chinese as it excluded her. I interviewed the girl in Chinese and it was clear she could understand what I said, though she was hesitant to reply in Chinese as she did not feel she could be sufficiently fluent. She said it was the first time for over a year that she had heard the language which she associated with the happiest period in her life, her early childhood spent with grandparents and extended family in Hong Kong. She showed me that she could still write her name and a few characters in Chinese. Over the past year no provision had been made to help her maintain links with the Chinese community, or to support her use of the Chinese language. She wanted to be able to read and write Chinese so that she could write to her family in Hong Kong. As they did not speak English, she could not otherwise communicate with them. She said she had not felt able to talk about any of this with either foster parents, social worker or psychiatrist, as they would not understand her wish to maintain a Chinese ethnic identity.

This case illustrates the difficulties in a professional system where the term 'Black' is applied to all ethnic minority groups, and thinking in child care derives solely from the paradigm of the historical conflicts between Whites and Afro-Caribbeans. It meant the child's ethnic identity needs, here tied in closely to positive hopes and aspirations for her future, were not addressed. An important therapeutic potential was therefore not mobilized.

In summary, I have found the following practice guidelines useful in the assessment of an ethnic minority family, and they may facilitate the task of 'working in partnership'.

1. What belief systems and value orientations influence role expectations, define and set limits of acceptable behaviour? For example, traditional Islamic views on family life provide for segregation of the sexes, especially after puberty, with the expectation of chaste behaviour for adolescents and virginity on marriage.

2. What are the structures relevant to authority and decision-making in the family? What are the kinship patterns? Which are the key relationships with important supportive functions? What is the relevant family network? Authority structures vary between groups but in the traditional Asian or Chinese family the concept of head of household is still important and authority may be vested in the most senior male member; often the paternal grandfather. The kinship pattern may be that of the traditional extended family, with the expectation of reciprocal obligations providing the basis of interconnecting family networks.

3. What life-cycle phase is this family at? What are the risks and challenges? What are the traditional solutions used to manage conflict and to what extent are they operational in this family?

4. Where does this family fit in the range from traditional/hierarchical to modern/egalitarian? How is the living unit organised to enable essential tasks to be performed?

5. What traditional networks and activities (based on religious or family ritual) maintain and support structural relationships in the family? Which of these have been lost, with what consequences?

6. What significant stresses and losses arise from the family's own experience, from the country of origin, from adaptation to the UK? What racial or cultural factors confer advantage or disadvantage to the individual/family in Britain?

For the traditional hierarchical Asian family the authority of the grand-parents and a close network of relatives may have maintained a protective and buffering function for its members, enabling conflicts to be worked through before tensions rise to intolerable levels. For other groups the authority of the church, or other religious organisations, may have served similar needs. Immigration to the UK and the loss of these networks may have contributed to increasing helplessness, especially in vulnerable individuals, in an environmental context where new rules are not well understood and communication, particularly language, is poorly established.

A couple from a traditional, hierarchical extended family background who have just undergone an arranged marriage would be in the life cycle phase of early marriage. Unlike their counterparts in the country of origin, they may not have the protection of extended family networks around them. In the author's experience, brides coming to the UK to join their husband's family, without ready recourse to their own families of origin, may be particularly vulnerable. It would be crucial for such a bride to form alliances with the network of female in-laws. Her relationship with mother-in-law would be especially important in determining her emotional survival in the extended family household, where initially she would be the most junior member in the 'family firm'. This often has implications for the emotional and physical well being of children in the marriage. The reader is referred to *Psychological Problems in Adolescents from Ethnic Minorities* (*Lau, 1990*) and *Family Therapy in Ethnic Minorities* (*Lau, 1988*) for a fuller discussion on differences in life cycle issues for ethnic minority families.

Assessment and treatment responses to significant harm must be sensitive to ethnic and cultural issues and enhance the potential for building a working partnership with families and communities. Practitioners should consider two further points to achieve these goals. They should ensure that their clinical hypothesis takes account of the meaning of the symptoms and behaviour presented as deviant from the family, the ethnocultural group and the wider social context, such as the school. They should also propose a strategy for intervention which attempts to mobilize strengths within a context that supports the authority structure of the family and community.

Bibliography

Henriques, F. (1949). West Indian Family Organisation. *The American Journal of Sociology.* **55(1)**: 30–37.

Henriques, F. (1951). Kinship and Death in Jamaica. *Phylon.* **12(3)**: 272–278.

Lau, A. (1984). Transcultural issues in family therapy. *Journal of Family Therapy.* **6**: 91–112.

Lau, A. (1986). Family Therapy Across Cultures. In Cox, J.L. (Ed.) *Transcultural Psychiatry.* London: Croom Helm, pp234–252.

Lau, A. (1988). Family Therapy and ethnic minorities. In Street, E., Dryden, W. (Ed.) *Family Therapy in Britain.* London: Open University Press, pp270–290.

Lau A. (1990). Psychological problems in adolescents from ethnic minorities. *British Journal of Hospital Medicine.* **44** September 1990: 201–205.

CHAPTER SEVEN:

Significant harm: the paediatric contribution

Margaret A. Lynch

This paper considers the contribution a paediatrician can make to the definition of significant harm and explores how paediatric evidence can also help the court decide whether or not all the threshold criteria for the making of a care or supervision order have been satisfied, including whether or not:

1. the child is suffering or is likely to suffer significant harm.

2. the harm is attributable to care given or likely to be given to the child.

3. the making of an order is better for the child than making no order.

These steps in the court process are compatible with the usual paediatric approach which should produce:

- an assessment of the child's condition (diagnosis);

- an opinion on the reason or reasons for this including attribution;

- advice on a management plan (treatment); and

- the likely prognosis.

Defining significant harm

The definition of significant harm is likely to be the focus of a long term debate, similar to that we continue to experience with the definitions of child abuse and neglect. This parallel makes it helpful to relate the definition of significant harm to the global definition of child abuse and neglect offered by Garbarino and Gilliam (*1980*): "Acts of omission or commission by a parent or guardian that are judged by a mixture of community values and professional expertise to be inappropriate or damaging". Such a definition allows for differences between cultures and over time, within cultures. It also offers the possibility that the definition of significant harm will similarly change with both shifts in community views and values and increasing professional knowledge. A definition combining community values and professional expertise implies the need for a continuing, constructive dialogue between the community and professionals: something that we have not yet satisfactorily achieved in this country.

In reality when considering individual cases professionals will continue to make value judgements on behalf of society. Often it will not be difficult to decide that significant harm is occurring. As will be discussed in more detail later harm can mean ill-treatment or impairment of health or development. Significant is defined in the dictionary as noteworthy, having considerable effect or importance. It also implies that some form of external assistance may be needed, at least to the extent of an investigation under section 47 of the Children Act. In many cases likely to come before the courts a 'reasonable' neighbour would be clear that a given child was suffering or was likely to suffer significant harm and, furthermore, that something should be done to stop the harm, for a child suffering recurrent physical or sexual abuse, a child whose health is obviously being neglected or a child who is left for a long period of time unsupervised. Intervention by professionals in such circumstances is likely to have community backing.

The need for 'intervention' criteria can also aid the paediatrician in her assessment. Where the consequences of ill-treatment or impairment of health or development have already, independent of any legal action, resulted in a referral to a paediatrician, there is a good chance that the child has a significant problem requiring treatment, i.e. has suffered or is suffering significant harm. The way in which the parents subsequently cooperate with treatment proposals may be crucial in deciding whether the child is likely to continue to suffer significant harm as the result of parental care. When the child is to be assessed medically for the first time because of an investigation by a social services department and the concern is impairment of health and development, there can be some advantage in initially using local screening services. If this is a child who the GP or clinic doctor would refer on to the paediatric department, child development centre, or other specialist resource, it is likely that this is indeed a child with a significant problem. This approach implies universally available screening services, willing to be involved in child protection and secondary paediatric services that are not resource led.

When in the course of a social services investigation an established problem usually warranting referral, for example chronic illness or severe developmental delay, is identified for the first time, it will be important to explore the reasons why the problem had not already come to professional notice. Those parents who have been failed by the system must be distinguished from those who have failed or actively refused to use local child health facilities. It will also be important to explore the extent to which the degree of any developmental delay is agreed as being 'significant'.

Factors influencing the paediatric contribution

The contribution a paediatrician can make to the decision making in an individual case will vary. It will never be more than one piece of a jigsaw puzzle to be assembled with contributions from the professionals and the family itself. Sometimes the piece of the puzzle brought by the paediatrician will be large while in other cases they will have no part to play. It is important for all involved in child protection to be able to consider critically the factors likely to influence paediatric opinion given to courts. Within paediatrics there are numbers of sub-specialities and the areas of expertise will vary between paediatricians. For example not all paediatricians will have been trained in the techniques of developmental assessment. The setting in which the child is seen will also influence the paediatric contribution. When I see a child for half an hour in the outpatients clinic my report is likely to be largely restricted to an assessment of health and physical development. On the other hand if I am able to spend an hour and a half in the child development centre, undertaking, often with the help of a speech therapy colleague, a full developmental assessment, my report will be wider and may well include comments on the child's behaviour and interaction with parents.

A paediatrician will also be influenced by additional direct or indirect knowledge that they have of the child. The child may already have been known to the paediatrician or valuable information may be available in past records. A local paediatrician might have treated other children within the family and have previous knowledge of the parents. This information should be shared and may well be valuable in predicting the likely outcome for the child. Some paediatricians like myself will find themselves increasingly involved with the second generation of families, being asked to assess children of mothers who themselves were known to us as children. This is clearly a very different position from one where we have just met the family for half an hour in the midst of a busy outpatients' clinic.

In addition to knowledge of the child and his family, our knowledge of the community and the culture from which the child comes is also very relevant. The paediatrician offering an opinion should acknowledge how much she does or does not know about the local community or of the culture from which the child comes. There should be a willingness to seek advice from those close to the culture concerned and we must be prepared to be honest about our own limitations. Paediatricians, like other professionals, will also have their prejudices. This means that sometimes in paediatrics, we will find examples of classism, sexism and racism. If it is felt that these or other prejudices are influencing a paediatric opinion, then other professionals must feel empowered to challenge the view being put forward.

Evidence of significant harm

Under the Children Act, significant harm means illtreatment or impairment of health or development. Both illtreatment and impairment are further defined as outlined earlier by White in Chapter 1. In most cases where illtreatment is alleged there will, in addition, be impairment of health and/or development. This may be a consequence of the alleged abuse or neglect, or be the result of more generalised failure in parenting.

It is to be hoped that in all cases, evidence of any impairment will be presented and that the outcome of the case will depend on more than proving or disproving the illtreatment. For this to be possible, information on every child's health and development will be needed, together with a willingness to modify the current adversarial approach which encourages, particularly in cases of sexual abuse, court battles focusing solely on the significance or otherwise of a physical sign.

Paediatricians will often have contributions to make to the diagnosis of both illtreatment and impairment of health and development. It will continue to be appropriate to call upon paediatricians to comment on evidence of physical illtreatment (abuse and neglect). This is an area in which, over the years, they have become increasingly more confident. They should be familiar with different patterns of inflicted injury, be able to detect inconsistencies between history and physical signs and symptoms. Experience should have made them familiar with the characteristics of the abusing parents' behaviour as well as that of the abused child. When asked to comment on the age of injuries it may be necessary for them to call upon a colleague, for example a paediatric radiologist when ageing bony injuries. Paediatricians should also be able to comment on evidence of physical neglect and define for the court what standard of care would be considered to be reasonable for a child of a given age.

The Act gives statutory recognition to the view that sexual abuse is illtreatment. Paediatricians will continue to have a valuable part to play in the assessment of suspected child sexual abuse but the limitations of their contribution and that of other doctors must be respected and understood, both within the professions and by society. Unlike physical abuse, the diagnosis can rarely be made on physical signs alone, and the absence of physical signs certainly does not equate with a false allegation. Furthermore it must be recognised that a medical training does not in itself provide knowledge of the normal and abnormal genital and anal anatomy of children of different ages. Even those of us who have worked with sexually abused children for some years need to acknowledge that we probably still have a lot to learn and are currently unsure of the significance of some physical signs. This means that we will not always be as certain in our opinions as colleagues, parents and courts would like us to be.

Illtreatment also includes abuse that is not physical; this means emotional abuse is included. Although this is traditionally thought of as an area more within the remit of the child psychiatrist, the paediatrician may also, in her contact with child and family, have observed examples of emotionally abusive behaviour. The paediatrician may additionally be able to provide evidence of the consequence of emotional illtreatment on the child's health and development by detailing the impairment that has resulted from the emotional illtreatment.

Paediatricians can appropriately be asked to comment on a child's physical health and development. In their assessment they should define any impairment and suggest the cause or causes. It is often easier to provide an opinion when data is available over a period of time rather than from an isolated encounter, for example the course of a medical illness or patterns of growth. With younger children the developmental paediatrician can also be expected to comment in some detail on wider aspects of the child's development, drawing on their experience of normal child development when judging as to the significance of any impairment. It will often be appropriate to ask for input from other members of a child development team such as the speech therapist, physiotherapist or psychologist. There is, for example, an increasing body of knowledge on the effects of abuse and neglect on language development. For the older child, the teacher is likely to have valuable information on the child's development and progress.

Paediatricians, as well as child psychiatrists, may have observations to make on a child's emotional and behavioural state and these should, when available, be included in any report. It is always important to comment on positive aspects of a child's health and developmental as well as highlighting problems. The extent of a developmental problem may only be apparent over time as may the contribution of parental care in its aetiology. Thus, not infrequently, it will be unrealistic to expect one isolated assessment to fully elucidate the extent of an impairment, its cause and prognosis.

In the process of assessing children for possible impairment of health and development it is likely that some children will be found who, while not suffering significant harm, will within the terms of the Children Act be 'children in need', that is, unlikely to achieve or maintain reasonable health or development without provision of services under Part III of the Act. The paediatrician as part of her assessment should include recommendations for the services needed to help the child overcome any present impairment or to prevent future harm. An opinion may then be needed from the paediatrician or other professional as to whether the parental attitude makes it likely that the advised intervention can take place without statutory intervention.

Past significant harm

The wording used in the Act allows for present and likely future harm but does not include past significant harm. (This does not rule out harm that was occurring at the time emergency protective action was taken but where the hearing for a longer term order takes place later). The importance of past significant harm will be its implications for future significant harm and the paediatrician may well be called upon to use her knowledge and experience to predict the likelihood of future harm in an individual case. This as we know may not relate to the severity of a previous injury. For example, a child seriously injured by a depressed mother, who has made a recovery and acknowledged her responsibility for the past harm, is much less likely to suffer future harm than the child with recurrent minor injuries inflicted by parents who refuse to see any need for their behaviour to change. Data does exist on re-injury and on neurological consequences of physical abuse. It would be appropriate to refer to such research when making a case for the likelihood of future impairment of health and development when commenting on both past and present abuse or neglect.

The question of a relationship between past and future harm will also be relevant when considering the welfare of children born to alcohol and drug addicted mothers. Both will have suffered demonstrable harm as the result of abuse *in utero*. However, the likelihood of future additional harm will be related to the continuation or otherwise of the addictive behaviour in the parents.

It must be remembered that past and present significant harm can both result in a child with a permanent disability and this must then be taken into account when assessing the child's future needs and the parents' ability to provide appropriate care.

The similar child and reasonable parents

The Act directs that "where the question of whether harm suffered by a child is significant turns on the child's health or development, his health or development shall be compared with what could reasonably be expected of a similar child" (*s31(10)*). As already indicated, the paediatrician should be able to give an authoritative opinion on what is considered normal healthy growth and development for a child of a given age. This should allow a comparison with the child under consideration to be made. We are, however, likely to see individual variations in the extent to which paediatricians and others will be influenced in their comparison by the culture, social background and living circumstances of families. Carers, including foster parents, can provide valuable observations on a child's development, including how she compares with a similar child. Same race foster placements will help us to learn more of expected development in different ethnic groups, as will discussions on child rearing and child development with natural parents of children seen in general and community paediatric clinics.

It is necessary to be cautious when using measures developed for children of one culture to assess a child from another. For example, growth charts in routine use were standardised on white children. This does not mean they cannot be used but care must be taken with interpretation. Indeed for any child a report of a single entry on a growth chart is of limited value. A child's height and weight must be put in context and related to parental size, prematurity and physical state. Information about growth monitored over time is of much more value and charts can then be used to plot the pattern for children of all races. The paediatrician should be sensitive to differences in motor development between different races, with the African child beginning to walk much earlier than the White European child. Enquiries should always be made about the languages spoken in the home. Sometimes a child is exposed to more than one, leading to different rates of progress in spoken English. We must acknowledge that English may itself be used with different structures.

For a child with an illness or chronic disability not primarily caused by abuse or neglect, comparisons will have to be made with children with similar special needs. Here too we can expect paediatricians to draw on experience gained in general paediatric practice.

The Act also requires us to make comparisons with the care a reasonable parent would provide for the child in question. Once again, we should expect the paediatrician to help define what this care should be for a child of a given age. For the child with special needs the paediatrician would have to consider the management plan that would be proposed to reasonable parents. The willingness and ability of parents to co-operate with the plan will then have to be explored. When considering prognosis, the expected outcome assuming reasonable parents should be compared with the likely prognosis given the level of care that the actual parents are able or willing to give. The extent of any discrepancy might well influence decisions over the necessity of an order. Children with special needs are often more dependent than children with normal health and development on the ability of their parents to co-operate with professionals. There may therefore be occasions when it will be necessary to make an order on a child with disability but not on other children within the same family.

Getting the paediatric evidence

Paediatric evidence falls into two areas: diagnosis and recommendation. The evidence is currently available from two main sources: local hospital and community paediatricians and 'second opinion experts'. It was hoped that implementation of the Children Act would be taken as an opportunity to encourage input from the first group and to re-appraise the position of the second.

The local paediatrician is likely to become involved in two main ways. Either she will already be seeing a child who then becomes the subject of legal proceedings or the child will be referred because of suspected abuse or neglect for an opinion on injuries or for an assessment of health, growth and development. Such a paediatrician with her local knowledge is well placed to take a global view of the child and family, who may already be well known to herself or her colleagues. She will know something of the community from which the child comes and be able to comment on local facilities available to the family. The potential evidence of such paediatricians must be given the consideration it deserves. Guardians ad Litem should request information from the local health services, even if they prefer to commission their own expert. Most local general and community paediatricians will attend court, but although they are usually called by the local authority, they see themselves as giving evidence in order to protect the best interests of their patient, the child, and will try to be fair and objective in their opinions. Not surprisingly therefore, they can be distressed by a heavily contested case with 'experts' brought in to discredit their opinions and even themselves, and they may become reluctant to repeat the experience.

While there is a need to ensure better training of general and community paediatricians in court procedures, report writing and presentation of evidence, attention must also be paid to the continuing demand for 'second opinion experts'. Not all of these experts are paediatricians and it is worth noting that neither the British legal or medical systems impose conditions or criteria on those doctors who set themselves up as medico-legal experts. It is particularly frustrating for those paediatricians who have for years examined and assessed abused and neglected children as part of their service provision to see greater credence given to opinions of 'experts' who may well have less direct clinical experience and no responsibility for comparable services.

There are ways in which, with encouragement from legal colleagues, cases can become less adversarial. As has already been pointed out the original examining doctor is unlikely, at least initially, to see herself as partisan. She would be willing to discuss, if given the opportunity, any alternative explanations for her findings. Consideration should always be given to whether it is possible to ask a paediatrician acceptable to all parties to undertake examination or assessment. It is to be hoped that those paediatricians best equipped to meet the challenges of the Children Act will be both willing and able to do so.

Bibliography

Augoustinos, M. (1987). Developmental effects of child abuse: recent findings. *Child Abuse and Neglect*, **11**: 15–27.

DHSS (1988). *Diagnosis of Child Sexual Abuse – Guidance for Doctors*. HMSO.

Garbarino, Gilliam (1980). *Understanding Abusive Families*. Lexington Books.

Law, J., Conway, J. (1992). Effect of Abuse and Neglect on the Development of Children's Speech and Language. *Developmental Medicine and Child Neurology*, **34**: 943–948.

Lynch, M.A., Roberts J. (1982). *Consequences of Child Abuse*. London: Academic Press.

Royal College of Physicians Report (1991). *Physical Signs of Sexual Abuse in Children*. London: RCP

Lynch, M.A. (1995). The Paediatric Role: Providing Assessment, Treatment and Continuity. In Batty, D. (Ed.) *Refocus on Child Protection: The Therapeutic Option*. London: BAAF.

CHAPTER EIGHT:

Making decisions in social work – persecuting, rescuing or being a victim

John Simmonds

Good judgement and quality decisions are two of the marks of the competent professional in any field. Several years ago, as the Children Act 1989 was being drafted and then implemented, social work was reeling under the enormous criticism levelled at it by the endless exposure of poor judgement and decision making contained in the child abuse inquiries culminating in the Cleveland Report (*Butler Sloss, 1988*). How was social work going to address its new responsibilities under the Act when so much of what was highlighted in reports was the poor judgement and decision making of social workers? While these inquiries often made recommendations which stressed the need for good information which is properly communicated and recorded, clear assessments and planning and a child centred approach, it seemed puzzling why, what from the outside seemed to be self evident, was in practice so difficult to achieve.

The concept of risk assessment appeared from time to time in these reports. Was there some more precise way of helping social workers bring the information they gathered into a formula that would pinpoint those children most at risk from those that were not? It was a recommendation made by Blom Cooper (*1985*) in one of the earlier inquiries – Jasmine Beckford – and he suggested research on the subject. This issue was worth exploring from the perspective of other professions who had a better track record in exercising judgement and decision making. Particularly interesting was the work that had been taking place to help casualty officers make better decisions about abdominal pain and the likelihood of this pain requiring surgical intervention for conditions such as appendicitis. The use of decision support systems, particularly the use of computers to aid this diagnostic decision making, seemed to hold exciting possibilities for social work in child protection. Although this preliminary research was fascinating, it was also rather shocking. In the first edition of this book some of the issues were outlined. One that continually stands out is the research on autopsies.

McGoogan (*1984*), performed 1152 autopsies to ascertain the accuracy of doctors' diagnosis of the condition/s that had resulted in the death of the patient. The doctors' certainty of diagnosis was categorised and then compared with the results of the autopsy. As Figure 1 shows, doctors were fairly certain in just under half of the 1152 cases and 75 % of these were confirmed at autopsy. A further 35% were categorised as probable and just over half of these were confirmed at autopsy. For a professional to be fairly certain in their judgement in 47% of their cases cannot be thought of as bad given the complexity of what doctors do and to be right 75% of the time might also be acceptable given this complexity. When we are told, however, that these errors of judgement were clinically significant and that if the course of treatment had changed, then the outcome for the patient might have been different, it is a matter of a quite different order. A number of other studies were reviewed in the original chapter which were indicative of the complexity of medical decision making and the risk of significant errors. In the end what was surprising was not so much the fact of this but the ability of the medical profession to hide this from public view and debate and create an image of certainty and infallibility.

If clinical decision making and judgement are difficult enough for the medical profession, it is unsurprising that they should be even more so for the social work profession, where decisions are made in the context of intimate human relationships, even if this can be seen in actual physical harm to children or the damage to their growth and development. Attributing meaning to the many ways abuse presents itself to child abuse professionals in order that they can develop an accurate and helpful picture about what has happened, why it has happened, and how it might be prevented and to make predictions about eventual

Clinicians certainty of clinical diagnosis	Cases certified clinically	Cases confirmed at Autopsy
Fairly Certain	47%	75%
Probable	35%	55%
Uncertain	16%	36%
Unspecified	3%	50%

Figure 1

outcome, is a task of a quite different order to the complexity that medical professionals grapple with. The objective of this chapter is to explore this, contrasting a typical model of the process drawn from management and current social work thinking with that which has a more dynamic perspective.

The numerous child abuse inquiry reports of the 1970's and 1980's provided clear evidence about the problems underlying poor judgement and decision making. Reder (*1993*) in a review of significant factors in 35 cases which had been subject to inquiries says "... workers often did not have available to them a framework within which to organise information and observations about the family or consider their implications". Although these reports highlighted many factors, two stand out. The first is the failure of professionals to adequately assess the risk to the child and continue to monitor that risk as the case unfolded. The second is the need to undertake a thorough assessment of the families' needs and circumstances and to plan for the child based on that assessment. The Children Act 1989 has prompted a number of developments that have attempted to put a more rigorous decision making and planning process in place – the *Children Act 1989 Regulations, Working Together* (*1991*), *Protecting Children* and *Looking After Children Materials.*

Assessment is the basis for good judgement and decision making and is at the centre of these developments. The principles of good social work require that any service delivered to clients should be based on a clear and proper formulation and assessment of that client's needs and circumstances. Although it is not popular to draw on medical analogies in social work, it is similar, in theory at least, to the idea of diagnosis and then treatment. This simple model has been given impetus in recent years by the introduction of care management thinking in social work (*SSI/Social Information Systems (1991)*). The recognition in this development that social work services were often delivered because, once established, they continued to exist and had to be used rather than because they were appropriate to a client's need raised many questions about the responsiveness, flexibility and efficiency of local authority services. As a result of this, the assessment of need separate from the delivery of services has become a central principle of social work policy through care management practice. Although care management principles have been primarily identified with services to adults, there has been a significant if variable amount of interest in it in respect of children and families. Even where the application of the purchaser/provider split as a primary mechanism for separating assessment from the delivery of services has not been instituted, the expectation that client's needs and risks will be assessed before they receive services is well established in social work thinking for all client groups.

The importance of assessment as a core activity in work with children and families cannot be denied. Identifying what needs to be done and why you are doing it and continually monitoring the effect should be easily identifiable from any case record where social workers are involved .

The process underlying this decision making model is readily found in literature from other disciplines. In a general management text, Adair (*1985*) identifies a clear logical and linear structure to good decision making practice. In summary, he defines this as those events (sense impressions) that indicate that a problem exists that needs a solution. This is followed by the definition of aims and objectives for the problem to be solved. A process of information gathering, the organisation of available data, identification of possible causative factors and the establishment of resource and time constraints follow as the next steps. The manager then needs to develop options for possible courses of action, listing the pros and cons in each case and testing and evaluating as necessary. Finally a course of action is identified which best meets the objectives.

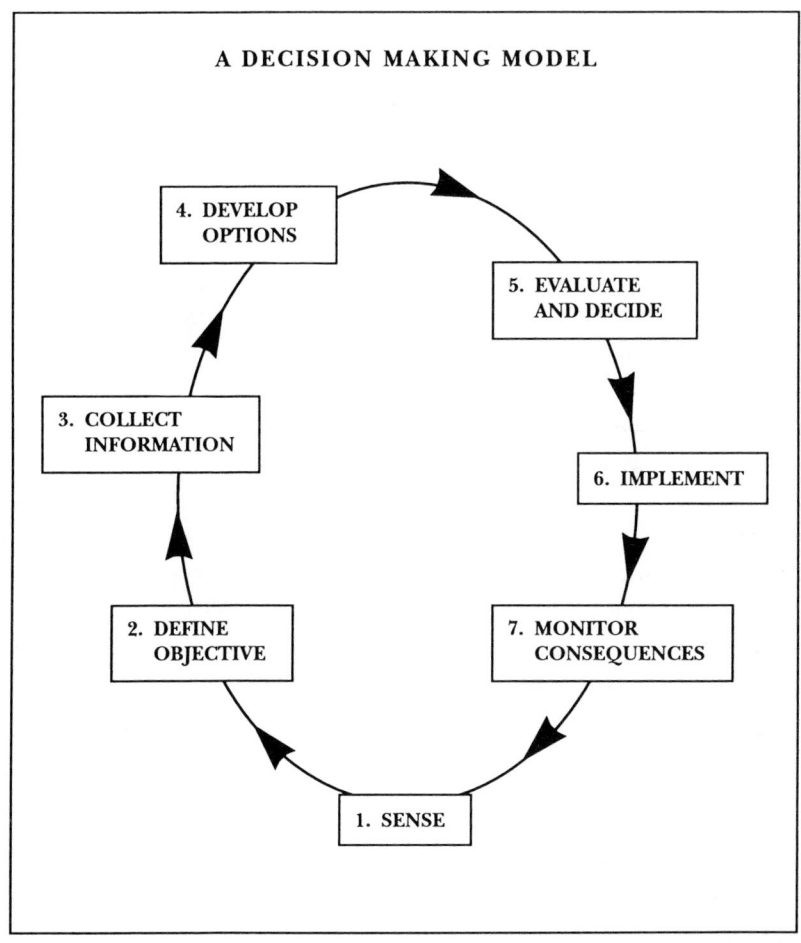

A DECISION MAKING MODEL

4. DEVELOP OPTIONS

5. EVALUATE AND DECIDE

3. COLLECT INFORMATION

6. IMPLEMENT

2. DEFINE OBJECTIVE

7. MONITOR CONSEQUENCES

1. SENSE

Figure 2

This is implemented, the effects monitored and reviewed. This model will be familiar to anybody in child protection who has followed procedures. As a model it cannot be argued with and probably there are many examples of poor decision making where such a process, thoroughly applied, would have improved the action taken and maybe averted disaster.

If we turn to the model of care management identified in the Department of Health's (*1991*) guidance, we find a similar model based on a circular process of assessment, planning, monitoring and evaluation.

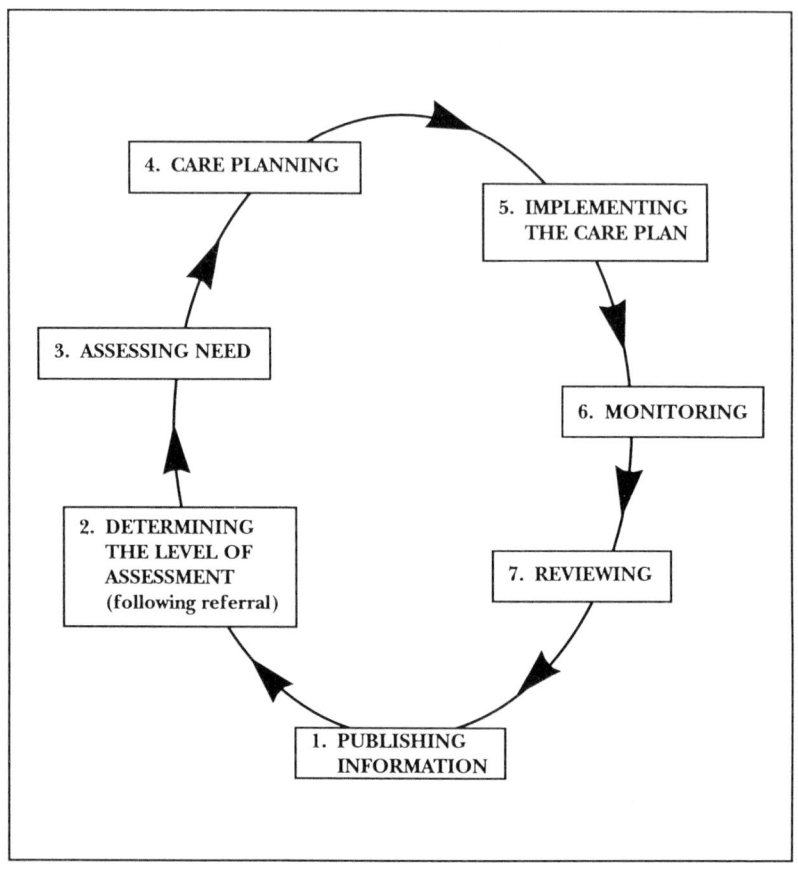

Figure 3

As powerful as these procedural models are, recent evidence from a number of inspections of child protection services (*SSI, 1993*) indicate that they are difficult to apply in practice. Further, the evidence of the Department of Health's research summarised in *Messages from Research* demonstrates that the efficacy of the child protection system in processing concerns might well be successful in managing publicly accountable risk but is not furthering the welfare of individual children and families who come into contact with it.

Gibbons (*1995*) in analysing the progress of 1888 child protection referrals of different kinds found that 14% were registered on the child protection register while just under 1625 families were diverted after investigation into either general monitoring of the child's welfare and limited practical support (56%) or into no further action (44%). Of this original group of non-registered children, a further 19% were reported for further harm within 6 months. Given the complexity of many child protection concerns and the management of risk within such a large group there is nothing surprising about these figures. But some important conclusions have been drawn from this. Even if the systems of decision making are successful in identifying those children where there is justifiable concern and eliminating those where there is not, successful risk management requires rather more for two reasons. The first is the often significant impact of being investigated on a family already stressed by factors of deprivation and disadvantage. The second is the fact that as a group overall, the research found it difficult to accurately distinguish the qualitative differences between abusing families and those that manifested the combined effects of multiple stressors – environmental, physical, social and emotional where the occasional abusive incident takes place alongside chronic disadvantage and deprivation.

What this research highlights is the particular difficulty of designing systems and models of risk management based on criteria and procedures that treat the problem as though it were testable by the procedures of science. Hamm (*1988*) clarifies this issue helpfully through his notion of the Cognitive Continuum (*see Figure 4*). (*See also Hammond, 1978, 1981, 1983.*)

This model of judgement is based on the interaction between two variables. The first variable he terms the cognitive mode which depends on the extent of the contribution of intuition to judgement and decision making as opposed to analysis. The second variable is the capacity of some tasks to being structured while other tasks can only be loosely structured. High degrees of structure are dependent on the possibility of the task being manipulated and its various components being both visible and capable of being measured. Figure 4 shows the interaction between these two variables with six possible models ranging from the scientific experiment in one corner to intuitive judgement in the other.

In exploring this continuum, it is possible to see the extent to which social work thinking has attempted to push judgement and decision

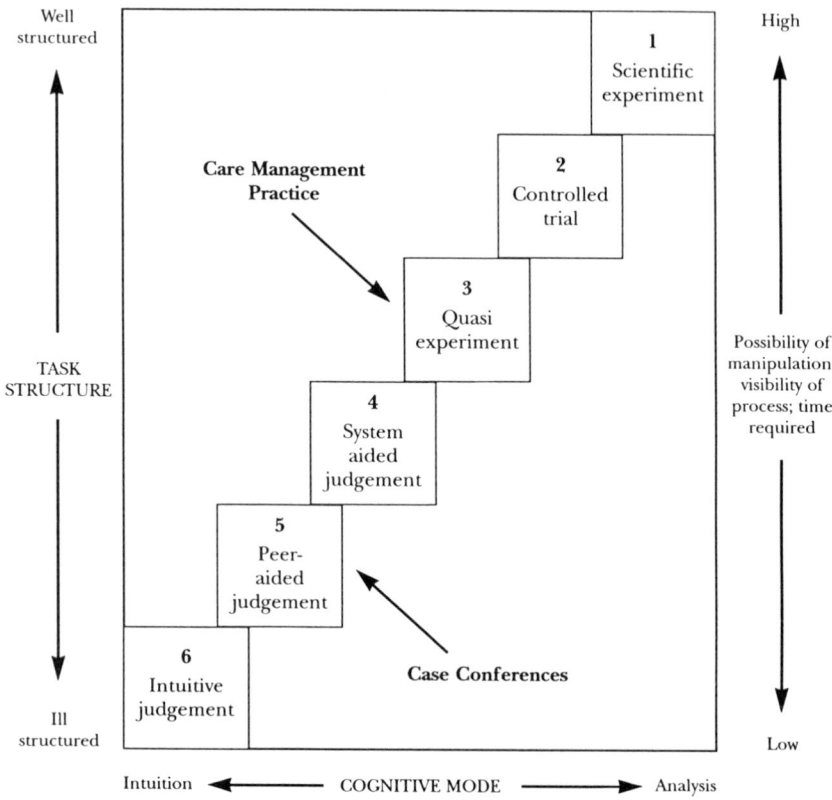

Well structured

High

1
Scientific experiment

Care Management Practice

2
Controlled trial

3
Quasi experiment

TASK STRUCTURE

Possibility of manipulation; visibility of process; time required

4
System aided judgement

5
Peer-aided judgement

6
Intuitive judgement

Case Conferences

Ill structured

Low

Intuition ← COGNITIVE MODE → Analysis

Hamm

Figure 4

making towards the quasi- experimental with developments such as care management. The concept of need in such models is assumed to be a variable that can be defined reasonably accurately and is therefore capable of being measured. The pro-forma used for assessment in care management are clear examples of this. The planning, monitoring and evaluation of the inputs are the steps in the experiment with needs being held constant and the effects of the inputs on these needs being measured. Whether human needs are capable of being worked with in this way is an important question although not answered directly here. The pro-forma designed for both community care and looked after children present a convincing argument for systematising client need in order that open and rational decisions can be made.

Case conferences in child protection are a good example of peer aided judgement where groups of professionals come together to systematically review available information to assess the risks to the child and produce a child protection plan. Aspects of this process are systematised through procedure and some parts of the process rooted in medical, legal and other forensic evidence but intuition plays its part at least in so far as this is acceptably defined as professional judgement.

Hammond's model poses some important questions about the beliefs that underpin professional judgement in terms of the structure of the task and its cognitive mode. The appeal of rational and highly structured processes discussed by Adair and very much in evidence in current practice models is very clear. However, managing 'sense impressions' (*Adair, 1985*) in social work requires a more complete understanding of what they mean than the immediate leap into assuming that they are best handled by the processes he and care management then identify.

Hughes and Pengelly (*1996*) adopt a more dynamic stance in identifying the forms that 'sense data' can take as unconscious or barely conscious feelings which give rise to feelings of anxiety or discomfort. The action of the human mind turns or modifies this anxiety into 'thought' which then becomes the basis of action to relieve the anxiety. This process is simple to describe but can be short-circuited to become what Hughes (*1996*) describes as a process of 'Jumping into Action'. Here, the unconscious or barely conscious feeling becomes the basis for direct action without these feelings ever becoming the basis for thinking. It is a process which is commonly termed 'acting out' or 'impulsive behaviour'.

JUMPING INTO ACTION

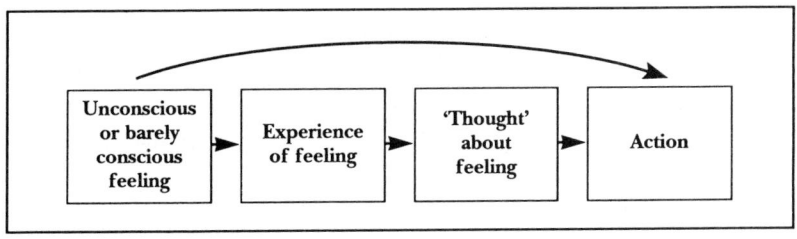

Hughes   *Figure 5*

The prototype of this process can be seen very clearly in the developmental immaturity of the infant mind which can be thought of as only capable of 'jumping into action'. Although the baby does not have the physical capacity to feed itself, it also does not have the capacity in its mind to turn the experience of hunger into a 'thought' which requires 'action' particularly where this requires language. As such, the raw experience of hunger has a primarily communicative function in relation to the baby's caretaker. A crying baby is unavoidable for most people in terms of the way it 'grabs' the attention of adults. The resulting relationship that this communication produces within the 'mind' of the caretaker, if it is sufficiently tuned in with or has empathy with the baby, is the means by which the baby's hunger is 'felt', 'thought about' and appropriately acted upon (*see Figure 6*). While this process is often hidden, it is through these experiences repeated numerous times and within the context of its developing maturity, that the baby's capacity to experience feeling as the basis for 'thought' and action is acquired. Fundamental to this is the caretaker's capacity for empathy involving the combined effects of receptiveness, attentiveness and responsiveness, qualities that define the capacity of the mind to engage in relationships with an ever widening world.

DEVELOPMENTAL PROCESSES IN RELATIONSHIPS

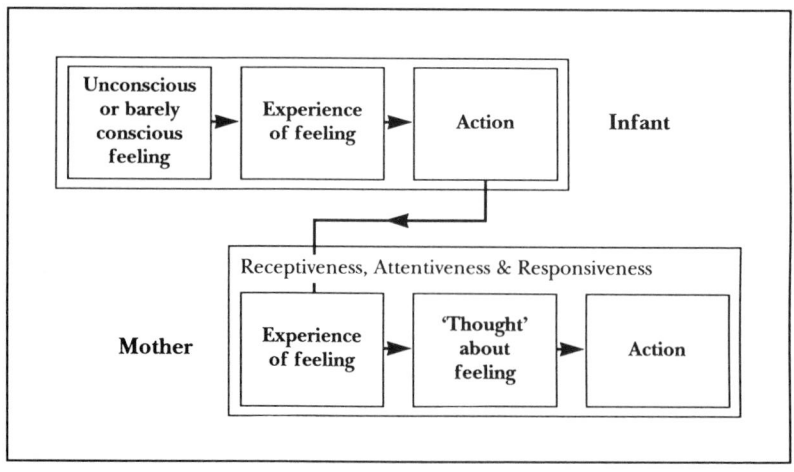

Figure 6

Attachment theory has paid particular attention to identifying the ways in which these early experiences become the basis for the individual's internal models of experience in relationships. These internal models can be thought of as containing five different elements.

- they are scripted in that they have a narrative which contains qualitative aspects of the relationship derived from the experience of the individual child with its caretaker/s.

- the script always has an element of reciprocity embedded within it – if X does this, Y will do that – which may or not be accurate but nonetheless is critical to the operation of the script.

- these scripts have both a conscious element to them such as the example just cited, and an unconscious element to them where the message has been coded in a deeper part of the mind. Here qualities such as receptiveness, attentiveness and responsiveness are embedded in the narrative as the context of these experiences.

- these scripts have a predictive power in that they both anticipate and construct the meaning of the individual's experience in relationships.

- these models contain powerful beliefs and values about the nature of the individual and the world in which they find themselves.

Although the model appears to have a straightforward linear progression to it, the experiences it continually gives rise to are constantly providing feedback as potential learning. However, because the models have also to be stable in order for them to be useful, there has to be a significant resistance to them being easily changed.

While the models individuals develop throughout their lives are unique to them in the sense that they contain the narrative scripts of their particular life experiences in relationships, there are also characteristics of these models which contain generic elements. Heard and Lake (*1997*) identify two of these generic elements. The first they describe as supportive/companionable and the second as dominating/submissive. Supportive/companionable relating "exemplifies a protective, explanatory and exploratory form of relating which owes as much to non-verbal signals and tone of voice as to communication through verbal symbols. It is a pattern to which people of all ages seem to be innately prepared to attend and to be influenced to adopt an exploratory stance. Conflict, when it arises, is handled by the recognition of the other's points of view and resolved through negotiation and compromise." The importance of the supportive/companionable dynamic to the processes described by Hughes (*1997*) are very clear.

Dominating and submissive forms of relating "force others to follow the decisions of a controlling leader. It can appear not to be damaging to others when it carries the stance of a protective and even indulgent dictator. But those who do not accept a submissive and obedient status face coercion in various forms, including being shamed and humiliated."

Heard and Lake (*1997*) also identify three basic partnership requirements of adults which they describe as caregiving/careseeking, interest sharing and sexual needs. Taken together this forms a matrix for understanding the characteristics of these internal working models of relationships in their script form for adults.

	Caregiving/ careseeking	Interest sharing/ Interest sharing	Sexual
Supportive/Companionable	1	2	3
Dominating/Submissive	4	5	6

Figure 7

The primary experiences which structure the caregiving/careseeking partnership are based in the attachment system in which individuals learn when things go reasonably well, that their signalling of care needs will bring about a supportive/companionable response from a caregiver. Over the course of a 'good enough' developmental history, the internalisation of caregiving and careseeking experiences within a supportive and companionable dynamic become established as the foundation of an internal supportive system and a pattern of relating to others with shared interests whether these are peer relationships, work relationships, or romantic/sexual relationships.

Dominating/submissive patterns of relating arise when the primary goals of the attachment system have not been met. The lack of a sufficiently attentive and responsive caretaker produces a pattern of relating which attempts as Heard and Lake (*1997*) describe "to secure what has been threatened or to restore what has been lost, with a minimum of further loss and distress. Individuals using the controlling pattern aim to safeguard themselves by influencing others, in one way or another, to become compliant and thus under their control. The use of compliance aims to minimise further loss by signalling the acceptance of control by the other. The cost is the suppression of anger and protest, and the curtailing of exploratory moves. It has profound effects on the sense of self-worth and effectiveness and the degree to which one values oneself."

Bentovim (*1996*) identifies the dominating/submissive forms of relating within the caregiving/careseeking relationship as the source of traumatic stress. This stress, he argues, leads to a pattern of traumagenic dynamics where the primary theme at the heart of the dominating/submissive pattern is powerlessness. The theme of power and powerlessness can be thought of as the deeply embedded outcome of a dominating/submissive pattern which when expressed within the context of a careseeking/caregiving relationship between parent and child can result in abuse. This in turn has a fundamental effect on developmental and interactional processes in the individual where, as Bentovim argues, the variables are gender, attachment patterns, direction of blame, identification and role and behavioural response. Embedded deep within the mind of the individual, they influence the way in which relationships are experienced, anticipated and patterned and, over time, become expressed generationally.

The narrative form of the scripts that are derived from these models is explored from a different perspective by Karpman (*1968*) in the 'Drama Triangle'. The inevitable vulnerability that arises through relating to others produces defensive scripts which Karpman identifies as consisting of three types. The first type is that of persecution, the second type that of rescue and the third type that of victimisation. Although each type is identifiable in its own right, it only exists in relation to the other two types. Under stress, individuals split off various aspects of these scripts and identify them in others. This results in a set of role relationships where each role exists as a defence against feelings which are associated with unbearable psychological pain. Karpman identifies the basic pattern of these relationships as a triangle.

The role of persecutor is a defence against vulnerability and the need for others that this would entail. These feelings are split off in phantasy and the vulnerability located in others – individuals or groups – who

MAKING DECISIONS IN SOCIAL WORK –
Persecuting, Rescuing or Being a Victim

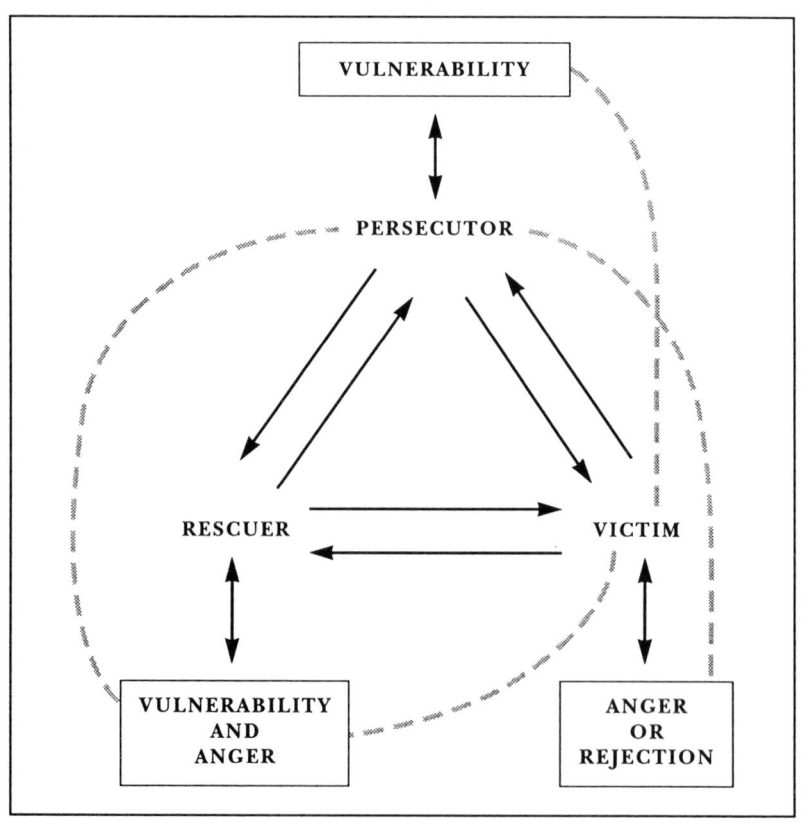

(John Simmonds)

Figure 8

become the victims to be treated with contempt for their needs. Bentovim (*1996*) identifies accompanying blaming and silencing strategies that are a part of such processes in child sexual abuse.

The role of victim is a defence against angry or rejecting feelings where these feelings are put into somebody who is then identified in the role of persecutor. The role of rescuer defends the individual against both their vulnerability which is located in victims and their anger which is located in persecutors. The defensive script for the rescuer is to save the victim from the persecutor.

This is a complex set of ideas and raises many questions that have rightly been put about the adequacy of systemic accounts of abusive relationships where an equality of responsibility is implied or seems to be assumed. Survivors of domestic violence or physical or sexual abuse whether children or adults cannot be held responsible or accountable for the abuse they suffer. But that they might be locked into complex patterns of relationships which need in some way to be brought to an end is one of the most daunting questions that they and others particularly in the helping professions have to face.

Karpman's (*1968*) Drama Triangle is a powerful sub plot to much literature, theatre and television. It can be identified in children's fairy tales and in the most complex and highest forms of art. The drama triangle describes the domination/submission dynamic and its defensive role in denying both the need for and complexities of the care-seeking/care-giving dynamic.

Decision making and professional judgement in this context takes on a quite different appearance especially when the primary focus of the task is care-giving as in social work. While this would suggest that the process is about people coming together (working in partnership) in cell 1 of Figure 7, in abusive families where the dominating/submissive dynamic pervades caregiving/careseeking, the most influential dynamic in the relationship between social worker as caregiver and client as careseeker will be derived from cell 4. 'Who dominates whom and for what end', becomes the basic script for the relationship whatever the intention on the part of the social worker to work within cell 1 and whatever the desire of the client to experience the work within cell 1.

When this also becomes the script for judgement and decision making, then the manifest content of the decision is constantly in danger of being subverted by the sub-script. While the models identified by Adair and others still have a relevance in structuring the process of judgement and decision making, there is another script which contains and maybe frequently structures how this process is understood and what purpose it serves.

The following example suggests that the script that powered the management of the case was other than what it appeared to be. In the example, significant questions arise as to how questions of power are resolved when professionals from different organisations come together to manage their care-giving arrangements. In particular, it raises questions as to how these organisations manage their own vulnerability – inadequate information, inadequate resources, poor communication, mistakes etc. in the context of engaging with a vulnerable child in providing care where fears of betrayal or exploitation were very powerful.

The case involves an adolescent boy of 13 whom I will call Paul. Paul had been seriously sexually abused in his family over a number of years. He had been removed from his family and placed with foster parents on a short term basis while a long term placement was found and a Care Order obtained from the Courts. The Order was secured but it took another three years to find a long term placement by which time he was firmly established with the original short term foster parents.

During this initial placement Paul displayed behaviour that was very challenging to the foster parents, his school and many other people who came into contact with him. He killed the foster family's pets with his bare hands, repeatedly stole food and money and was threatening to the foster parents' children. His progress at school was erratic although he was assessed as above average in intelligence and he had great difficulty in maintaining friendships. Despite these difficulties, he could be charming, warm and humorous and he had developed a close relationship with both his foster mother and father. Psychiatric assessment and psychotherapeutic help were provided for Paul during these three years and did have the effect of providing him with an additional measure of containment. The stresses on the foster family were understandably intense given the length of time it was taking for the local authority to find a new placement. There were genuine difficulties in finding a suitable family but the length of time started to cause a rift between the local authority and the foster parents until eventually the relationship broke down as any kind of constructive working alliance.

The practical strains of such a situation when fostering resources are scarce and the original placement agreement has been stretched to breaking point are real enough. It is difficult to find a way of providing the young person with a clear sense that adults are able to come together to make decisions and plan in order to create a secure physical and emotional space for the necessary work of attending to his powerful anxieties and needs. Paul brought into care powerful feelings of loss, distrust, anger and betrayal resulting from the perversion by his father of a supportive/companionable script in the careseeking/caregiving parental dynamic to a dominating/submissive script. Despite the foster family's overt commitment to protect Paul from his past and nurture him into a healthier future or to replace this perverted script with an appropriate caring script, the underlying issues were quickly communicated to them through Paul's behaviour. While the emphasis in the foster placement was in providing a secure careseeking/caregiving dynamic, the damaged and damaging script needed to find an outlet somewhere in order that the foster family and Paul could have some sense of being protected from the destructive impact of these feelings. The local authority social workers became the obvious receptacle for these feelings where their genuine difficulties in placement provision and their vulnerability in relation to this task were interpreted by the foster parents to be the result of secrecy, neglect, lack of concern if not outright abuse of their commitment to Paul. The accusations and tension that resulted from these powerful feelings overwhelmed the professionals involved. Communication between the foster parents and the local authority became dominated by anger, misunderstanding and apparent intransigence.

The foster parents became identified with the young person's plight and used it to attack the apparent inability of the local authority to do the necessary work to find a placement. The local authority became identified with the negligent parent, feeling overwhelmed about the demands being placed on them, while in a state of deprivation and poverty in relation to their own resources. The Drama Triangle was complete – from the foster parent's perspective, there was a victim in Paul's role, a rescuer in their role and the local authority were identified as the persecutor. From the local authority's perspective, they felt the foster parents to be the persecutors, themselves to be the victims of unreasonable demands when they were trying, against the odds, to be the rescuer of Paul by finding a long term placement. In other scenes, Paul was the persecutor of the foster family and indeed murderer of the family's victim rabbits, where the foster family pleaded with the social worker to rescue them from his violent actions.

Decision making and good judgement in such circumstances is extremely difficult, indeed it is hard to know quite what one might mean by the term 'good' in such circumstances. Any attempt to exert some control over these events and follow a rational model only seemed to fuel the unfolding drama.

When eventually a new foster family was secured, Paul was very keen to go to the new placement to the relief of all concerned. Because the dynamics identified above had become firmly entrenched, the communication and decision making involved in planning this move was poor. It was carried along largely by Paul's enthusiasm as he appeared to be rescuing the local authority from their victim role and relieving the foster parents of that aspect of his placement where they felt themselves to be a victim of his challenging behaviour. All the scene needed was a persecutor.

None of the parties could escape from their assigned script to feel sufficiently secure to acknowledge the very real feelings of loss and danger in this move. Whatever difficulties there were in the original placement, it was secure and the relationships were meaningful to both the foster parents and to Paul, even if this was at the expense of the serious breakdown in the relationship with the local authority. Rather than finding space to have 'thoughts' about these feelings, the system jumped into action, as though action could take the place of thoughts based on inevitable feelings of loss. 'Being enthusiastic' about the new placement was seen as the ideal if not idealised solution to a painful set of circumstances that deeply troubled all the parties to this drama. This might be thought of as a repeat of the original unbearable traumatic stress in Paul's family of origin.

On the first day of the new placement Paul became disturbed and violent with his new foster parents whom he quickly identified as persecutors despite their earlier identification as rescuers. He rang his old foster parents pleading with them to rescue him. Distressed at what they were hearing from him and the new foster parents, who felt Paul was demonic, they agreed immediately. That night, with the local authority looking on in helpless despair, he returned to the first foster placement.

While this tragic move was rescued by the care of the first foster parents and their refusal to abandon this young person in a desperately escalating situation, it is important to recognise that this event was dominated by an overwhelming sense of anxiety where no adult – local authority social workers, old or new foster parent, or other professional could provide a strong enough sense that whatever the young person's fears about the move, they were understandable and most particularly were not annihilating. It may of course be unreasonable to expect that any one person was capable of playing such a role but arguably that is the advantage of professionals coming together to pool their joint emotional resources to support one another in such circumstances. In this situation however, different people represented or were identified with different scripts in the process of change but were so locked into the drama triangle behind their organisational roles and boundaries that they were unable to bring these perspectives together either in planning the move or implementing it in a way that was tolerably safe for the young person concerned.

The effect of this crisis was to cement even further the sense of powerlessness and fear on the one hand and distrust and betrayal on the other. The decision that was eventually made was to undertake a period of assessment in a therapeutic residential unit. A referral was made to such a Unit and a contract was drawn up that an introductory assessment would be made while Paul continued to live with the foster parents to be followed, if the Unit agreed, by a longer period in residence.

A number of day visits were arranged over the first few weeks to be followed by a number of overnight weekend stays. Initially the visits went well. Paul was extremely enthusiastic about the Unit. He liked the staff and was excited to be in the company of other adolescents. After the first visit he said he liked the Unit so much, he wanted to pack his bags and move straight away. This continued through the second and third visits until after the fourth visit, he returned to his foster parents complaining that somebody was trying to poison him at the Unit. He also felt that one of the children was trying to have a sexual relationship with him when they kissed him goodbye. From this point Paul refused to visit the Unit any further despite attempts to reassure him. His behaviour both at the foster home and at school became more withdrawn or more demanding. The foster parents reacted to this increased anxiety by attacking the local authority social workers for their failure to manage his admission to the Unit and so the cycle of the Drama Triangle was in danger of beginning again.

It would be tempting to identify how Paul was rescued from this situation. However, it seems clear that the different parties needed to get out from underneath the dramatic scripts that were acting defensively to prevent them from taking charge of Paul's placement. In order to do this they would need to work co-operatively within a supportive/companionable dynamic that could contain the real anxiety that each felt about the responsibility of their own role.

The principles of what needed to be understood in order to make better decisions about managing this complex situation are clear. The facts needed to be gathered but were not contained in any needs assessment of Paul or re-statement of Paul's history or a comprehensive assessment or looked after children pro-forma, although they existed in Paul's file. What did need to be recognised is that the system of relationships that held Paul in care was being energised by the unbearable pain of Paul's relationship with his family and particularly his abuser. He had been the object of his father's defensive acting out where feelings never became turned into thoughts, painful or anxiety provoking as they might have been. Thoughts never became held in the calming mind of an attentive and responsive adult. The system of relationships between Paul, his foster parents and the local authority was driven by uncontained anxiety where the supposed control of rational decision making only fuelled guilt, blame, secrecy, rage and despair around the drama.

This poses us with a significant challenge. The challenge is not in devising more and more sophisticated pro-formas and procedural mechanisms for gathering information but of attending to something which we know about but maybe have greater difficulty in attending to – that social work is about managing decisions that are often driven by unbearable impulses and feelings. The challenge is in developing a state of mind that can bear to develop an awareness of these processes as they operate not just in individuals but across systems. They require us to act without ' jumping into action'. Above all they require us to use our authority so that needs and the anxieties that accompany them can be acted on not acted out. This requires that particular quality of thinking, feeling and professional judgement that adequately recognises the traumatic origin of events involving children and adults with whom we work.

This is a revised version of a paper given at an NSPCC conference in Autumn 1997.

Bibliography

Adair, J. (1985). *Effective Decision Making, A Guide to Thinking for Management Success.* London: Pan.

Adcock, M., White, R., Hollows, A. (1991). *Significant Harm.* Croydon: Significant Publications.

Bentovim, A. (1995). *Trauma Organised Systems.* London: Karnac Books.

Blom-Cooper (1985). *A Child in Trust.* London Borough of Brent.

Butler-Sloss, Lady Justice E. (1988). *Report of the Inquiry into Child Abuse in Cleveland 1987.* London: HMSO.

Department of Health (1988). *Protecting Children: A Guide for Social Workers undertaking a Comprehensive Assessment.* London: HMSO.

Department of Health (1995). *Looking after Children, Trial Pack.* London: HMSO.

Friedman, C.P., Purcell, E.F. (1983). *The New Biology and Medical Education: Merging the Biological, Information and Cognitive Sciences.* New York: Josiah Macy, Jr. Foundation.

Gibbons, J., Conroy, S., Bell, C. (1995). *Operating the Child Protection System.* London: HMSO.

Hamm, R.M. (1988). Clinical Expertise and the Cognitive Continuum. In Dowie, J. and Elstein, A. (1988). *Professional Judgment: a Reader in Clinical Decision Making.* Cambridge: Cambridge University Press.

Hammond, K.R. (1978). *Judgment and Decision Making in Public Policy Formation.* Boulder: Westview Press.

Hammond, K.R. (1978). *Toward increasing competence of thought in public formation in Hammond.*

Hammond, K.R. (1981). *Principles of Organisation in Intuitive and Analytical Cognition (Report 231),* Boulder: University of Colorado.

Hammond, K.R. (1983). *Teaching the New Biology: Potential Contributions from research in Cognition in Friedman,* (1983).

Heard, D., Lake, B. (1997). *The Challenge of Attachment for Caregiving.* London: Routledge.

Home Office (1991). *Working Together under the Children Act 1989.* HMSO.

Hughes, L., Pengelly, P. (1997). *Staff Supervision in a Turbulent Environment.* London: Jessica Kingsley.

Karpman, S. (1968). Fairy Tales and Script Drama Analysis. *Transactional Analysis Bulletin,* 7(26): 39–44.

McGoogan, E. (1984). The Autopsy and Clinical Diagnosis. *Journal of the Royal College of Physicians of London,* 18: 4.

Medical Aspects of Death Certifications (1982). *A Joint Report of the College of Physicians and the Royal College of Pathologists,* 16(4).

Parker, R., Ward, H., Jackson, S., Aldgate, J., Wedge, P.(1991). *Assessing Outcomes in Child Care.* London: HMSO.

Reder, P., Duncan, S., Gray, M. (1993). *Beyond Blame: Child Abuse Tragedies Revisited.* London: Routledge.

SSI (1991). *Care Management and Assessment, Practitioners' Guide.* London: HMSO.

SSI (1993). *Evaluating Child Protection Services: Findings and Issues, Inspections of Six Local Authority Child Protection Services 1993: Overview Report.* London: HMSO.

SSI/Social Information Systems (1991). *Assessment Systems and Community Care.* London: HMSO.

Ward, H. (1995). *Looking After Children: Research into Practice.* London: HMSO.